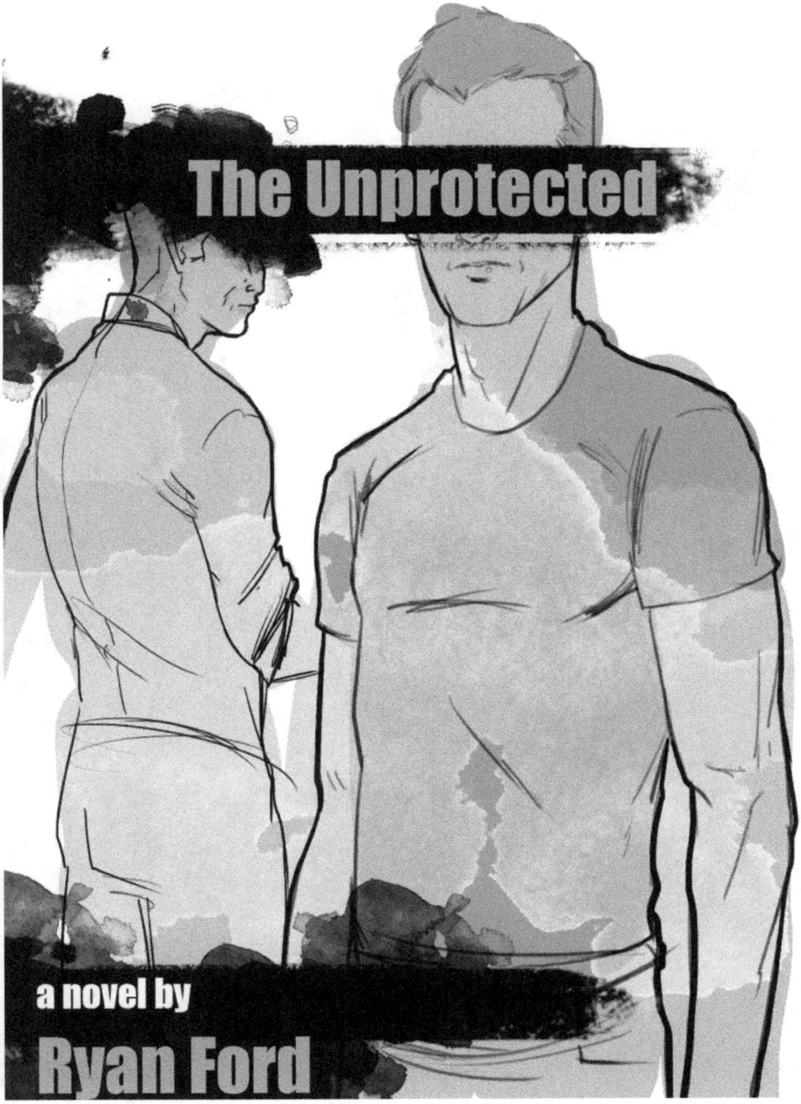

The Unprotected

a novel by

Ryan Ford

The
Unprotected

By
Ryan Ford

Dedicated to and in remembrance of:

Michael James Dunkley

The days we spent together were amazing, the nights even better. The idea of losing you was a long time coming and there was only so much I could do. I could have done more to prevent this horrible tragedy, and stop this horrible act. But at that time I did as much as I knew I could. This was unpreventable by me alone, but as a whole it could have been prevented. As a community, a state, a religion, and simply as a group of human beings this could have been prevented. If we as a society would accept the teachings of tolerance and acceptance, and not only learn, but listen and live the teachings we all preach in our sermons, and our daily lives. If we learn to love the individual for whom they are as a person and being, and not hate against them for what we believe are sins, trespasses, mistakes, wrong choices, and disagreements which you may have against them for who they are or what they are doing. But instead understand that people are people, different, unique, and individualistic. If they weren't, what a horrible world it would be. The pain I have felt from losing you from this world is unreal, unnatural, unfair, and unchangeable. As a man who shared many aspects of your life with you and day by day sharing and connecting with you even more. I will fight, brawl, argue, yell, and claw my way to promote equality and equal rights. Not only to become equal but to become more accepted, loved, cared for and tolerate; to lessen the torment, the persecution, and the anger against us. In doing this I hope to prevent feelings of inadequacy, second class, and unwantedness, lowering the awful thoughts of hopelessness and suicide. My love for you is firm and unchanging. Until the moment when I run back into your arms, holding you and gracing my hands upon your body, I will fight for this cause. For you and for every other person that has ever and will ever feel the sorrow you have felt because of discrimination. For the people that are affected by these suicides like I have been from you and your unnecessary passing. For the hope and love that could have been if even just one life had not ended premature. I will stand up and fight for you and every other man woman and child that intolerance has affected, and that I promise you Michael James Dunkley. The thoughts of you have always and will always be with me until my end. When my job is complete, and my end is handed to me, along with my end will be our beginning.

Love always,

Ryan Ford

Chapter 1

Taylor lies lifeless on the floor physically and emotionally exhausted. Not knowing where he was; wondering why he couldn't move. He hollers out in agony as pain shot up and down his body, reminding him of the times the dentist chiseled the last remaining decay in a cavity, scraping and grinding it down to the core. The scream out of his throat had no noise; no sound. Was he dead? His body would not move. Feeling entirely numb, Taylor tired to move again, still nothing. I'm paralyzed, I must be; Taylor thought to himself, but why?

Taylor thought how long have I been here? Wherever here is, he ponders trying to make sense of it all. For another fifteen minutes or so he rests motionless in excruciating pain. Piercing his eyes a ray of light managed to make it through a very small crevasse between his eye lids. The light was the brightest light that he had ever seen. "I must be in heaven, he thought. Ha! I made it in, despite what everyone said about my life, that I was screwing it up and ruining the family name. I'm in! I have accomplished my biggest goal in life." The light still blinding him as he started to speculate; "was there going to be a big reunion? Would all my family that had passed away come out and greet me at the pearly white gates and welcome me into heaven? Maybe this was not heaven," he wondered.

As time passed, the light became more tolerable, although very slowly like a paper plane gliding down toward the street, after being thrown off the roof. It started shrinking. Getting smaller and smaller till it was only a dot; a hole, in what looked like a gray surface, a wall possibly. By the time his eyelids opened the wall was coming into focus. The compositions of the bricks were much bigger than he had originally thought. More of a cinder block size than an average house brick. He came to the assumption, the light now in total alignment, it had to be a tiny little window located at the top of the wall. Just big enough to give a minimal amount of light to the space he was in; still not exactly sure where he was.

Taylor forced his dry eyes open, realizing he may have injured his retina; he squeezed them shut with just as much friction as trying to ice skate on an overly used gravel road. With the discomfort from closing his eyes lingering, he felt additional pain in his body. He moved his pupils back and forth to obtain liquids that have drained to the side, his body still inactive on the floor. With substantial amount of liquid now smeared on the inner side of his eyelids, he opened his eyes again. This time a little faster and with a little less energy. Still hurting from the first time he scratched his eye, the light came back into focus, not as striking this time. The window appeared clear and the brick wall shortly followed. He noticed the wall had to have been deeper than he had originally imagined, for he could not see through the window to the outside. All he could see was the light beaming in through the window. The light shot across the room. Seeing dust particles floating through its rays, he stared at them for the longest time until he saw movement on the floor not too far away.

Taylor blinked to make sure it was actually there, squinting to see more clearly. Its movement stalled for a moment; moving its head to look at him. Staring him in the eyes, motionless for just a few moments, then back to what it was doing slowly across the frozen dusty floor. Taylor followed it with his eyes, trying not to make a sound, and then realized that he could not, even if he wanted to. Taking a few steps and stopping; then a few more making sure with every pause it had enough time to look around to check its surroundings. It finally came close enough, still being a few feet away, that Taylor could make out what it might be. A small rodent of some sort, a rat or mouse possibly. After a few more pauses, his eyes rolled farther and farther up till the rodent moved out of sight past the top of his head. He listened for movements; a long pause. It came back into focus running without stopping; as fast as it could, back into the hole in the wall it had originally come from.

"Exactly where am I?" Taylor wondered as he looked back at the small window which had managed to allow some sunlight through. Being so fixated on the rodent, he did not realize how much pain had
actually left his body, wondering why it was even there. Giving one more shot at moving his body, he mustered up his energy and forced himself to push all he had left into this one simple motion. He was surprised by the energy he had, as his arm propelled slightly up, then fell back to earth's surface. By this time, he had enough mental capacity to realize that he was probably not in heaven; unless heaven was a horrible place, which he hoped would not be the situation. Taylor thought "I did not struggle all my life to be perfect, just to get into heaven and have it look like this. With this not being heaven could it possibly be hell? Was I really cast down into damnation?"

A few moments and situations of his life flashed back into his memory, had these few mistakes he had made really been enough to prevent him the joys of the hereafter? Maybe it was; but it was not how he would have imagined damnation being. Not hot enough, no fiery hot furnaces smoldering with burning coals and dead white ash. No fire and brimstone. Knowing that he was not being greeted in heaven and this place did not look or feel like how he envisioned hell, he assumed that he must not be dead. Taylor questioned again, "Where could I be? Not a very luxurious place, that's for sure." He forced himself to fling his arm upward faster this time; staying in motion a little longer until it came crashing down on his side and ending up on the hard frosty floor. He could feel more energy slowly flourishing throughout his body, running through his veins, and pulsating his arteries like he imagined your hands do while donating blood. He had never actually been able to donate blood himself due to rules and regulations. "Hell, if they don't want my blood, they don't have to have it," he thought.

With his eyes moistened enough now to be functioning correctly; he noticed the eyes from the bottom of the wall staring back at him; wondering why he was in his home. Two beady little pupils staring at him like he had taken something that belongs to him. He must have seen Taylor's second attempt to raise his arms because he refused to come back out of the dark hole in the wall. Without his authorization his finger twitched, grabbing his attention. Taylor's heart raced uncontrollably; he did not know what to do. "Was there even anything I could do?" He thought. He still had minimal control over his body and its movements. The twitching slowed. Coming to a stop, he moved his hand downward, palm now flat against the floor. Still extremely weak, he mustered up some energy and pushed with all his might; he managed to lift himself a few inches off the ground, when his arm gave out careening him back toward the floor, causing his face to smash against the concrete bringing unbelievable pain, not only to his face, but throughout his entire body.

Being able to move his arm slightly, he reached toward his face to see why there was so much pain from the short fall. Taylor felt a wet substance pooling around his face. Not knowing what it could be, he pulled his hand into sight to examine what

4

was on it. It was too dark to really tell anything. He forced his hand downward to his shirt hoping that if it was blood, there would be a stain visible on his shirt. The liquid printed a mark of some sort not dark enough to be blood. He moved his hand back toward his face, dipped it back into the substance and brought it to his nose, accidentally rubbing the liquid onto his nose. Taylor inhaled, gagging at the smell, the liquid reminded him of his child's breath when she had the flu, in December a few years back. Taking a few breaths to exhale the wretched smell out of his lungs, he placed his palm face down on the concrete and attempted to push himself up again. With his right arm still refusing to assist in the process, Taylor managed to drag his lifeless body to the wall with the help of only his left arm.

Propping himself up next to the rodents home, he takes a deep breath, and then thrusts it out. He was glad to be out of the pool of stench he was in for who knows how long. Sitting up, recuperating his breath and energy. Still in pain, Taylor looked around managing to move his head to see the walls surrounding him. He was in a room; a small room at that. All the walls were made out of the same cinderblock sized brick. Smooth to the touch, he stroked the wall till his fingernails pressed against the floor, bending slightly. Looking down, as his pants rode up a little, neither of his socks matched, which surprised him. "I'm so obsessed with always having my socks match," he thought. Leaning forward he pulled off the unmatched sock realizing he was missing a shoe as well. He threw the sock across the room, left-handed, with it not going where he wanted it to.

Bringing his hand up toward his forehead, he rubbed it and scratched his tangled hair, trying to remember what even happened before he ended up in this place. Taylor heard a man's voice in the distance yelling something incomprehensible to him. He looked around wondering where the sound was coming from. He couldn't see anyone else with him. "Hello" he mumbled out. Clearing his throat he tried again. "Hello" he shouted a little louder sounding very raspy. Swallowing a few times trying to moisten his mouth preparing for another attempt; hoping for an answer but not knowing what he would get. "Hello" he burst out once more, with more authority than before, still nothing.

In the distance he could faintly hear a squeaking sound. The noise intrigued him; he wondered if the high pitched squeaking was coming from the rodent. Not being a rodent enthusiast, actually hating them himself, he had no idea. After a few moments of silence, the sound again protruded through the walls. Then it stopped once again. He heard the mumbling of a man's voice; a little louder this time, but still unrecognizable. The mumbling voice lasted a little longer this time with only a few very short pauses in between, like a conversation. Still focusing on the voices, the thought of there being more than one person flashed through his head briefly, not knowing if that was a good thing or not. The voices stopped simultaneously. "What the hell could it be, or who the hell could they be?" Taylor questioned.

Taylor was still propped up in a sitting position against the wall. The squeaking sound began slowing to a stop. What could the person possibly be doing on the other side of the wall? Taylor thought. A latch at the base of one of the walls flew open splashing a bright light throughout the small room, blinding him once again temporarily. A low but burly voice, said "Tray." The light shinning in letting him see the whole room. Taylor quickly shot his head around the room to get a better visual of where he was. The walls were brick just as he had thought, making sense of why they were smooth, paint; they were all painted white from the ceiling to the floor. He looked back at the latch that had been opened now able to see through to the other side of the wall.

Taylor stared through the bright light gazing at the objects on the other side appearing to be the outline of a shoe. "Hello? Sir?" He yelled. The response came abruptly "Gimme your tray." "What?" Taylor said still confused. "Where am I?" he asked. "Just gimme your tray," the grungy deep voice said once more. "What tray?" Taylor mumbled confused at what he had just heard. Looking quickly around, Taylor saw a tray with some gray looking food splattered on it. He lunged forward to push the tray out of the hole that was now fully open, falling down landing in front of the tray his face almost landing upon it. Forgetting that he still could not move his legs, he pulled himself closer to the door with his left arm, propping himself against the wall. Sitting next to the latch, he pushed the tray slowly to the outside, expecting to have more food placed on it upon its return. A few moments later the tray reemerged sliding back in about half way across the small room. The foot-steps and squeaking started up again at about the same time. The sound became faint. Stopping and starting every few seconds. Probably giving food to the others as well, or so Taylor assumed.

"Why was I getting food? Why was I in this small room unable to move?" Taylor thought, even more confused now. Remembering all of the things he went through in junior high and high school that he was confused about, none of which compared to this moment. He recalled going out into nature to kneel down and pray to God asking, "Why me? Why me? Why do I have to be challenged by this? Why can't I just be normal? Why can't I just stop being teased and patronized? Going through the worst school experience and having my entire family look down on me. Losing my friends when I told them I had been lying to them all of these years. Remembering all the times my family told me that I was pursuing a life that would only bring me unhappiness and sorrow. I remember it all so clearly. Thinking

7

about at least part of it on a daily basis; trying still to this day to get the answers I pondered so much as a child, why me? I have come up with many possible explanations not knowing if any are the correct one. I guess I will never know, until I can ask God himself, if I make it there." Taylor questioned.

The latch was still open giving the room an abundance of light. Taylor took advantage of it and grabbed the spoon off the floor and shoved his mouth full of the gray filth slathered on his tray. Eating as fast as he could, not realizing how hungry he actually was until it was about gone. Taylor wished he would have not eaten it so fast. It was the fastest he had eaten since he and his brother would go out to eat with his dad when they were kids. Making Taylor leave the restaurant as soon as they were done if he was done or not, he had learned to eat fast or not eat at all. His eyes began to tear a little remembering all the good times they had together growing up. Until he told them his secret and they disowned him forever. Never to talk to him again; no phone calls, no letters, nothing.

Until about five years ago Taylor had never before received a call from his brother. He never told him how he got his number; Taylor could only guess. Maybe off one of the letters he had sent; online perhaps. He just settled with the fact that he will never know. "I called you just to say sorry." His brother said as he started the very short conversation. "Sorry for what? Who is this?" Taylor interrupted. "Stephen, your brother" he said in a confused tone. "I just wanted to say sorry for abandoning you all those years ago, for never contacting you; for not being a real older brother; for doing nothing really. I just called to say I'm sorry and ask for forgiveness." Click. He had hung up. Taylor saw his obituary in the paper five days later, after getting hit by a large stroke; Gods way of saying I need you, come home. The following weeks were some of the hardest Taylor had ever gone through. Not going out of the house or even getting out of bed, except to use the restroom and eat occasionally. Lying there in bed just thinking about his family. Trying to put his head around how they could abandon him like they did. That is something he could never do to his family, no matter what his kids told him or did. He promised he would always love them as if he were proud of them even if he was not.

Taylor grabbed his shirt to wipe the tears from his eyes, and the ones that were dripping down his cheeks, as he finished his food. Again he tried moving his right arm, praying with all sincerity, that it would move, drops of sweat permeated through his pores on his forehead just below his hair line. Seeing no movement, he let out a significant amount of air. Not realizing it, he had pulled both of his legs into a sitting position, or as his children would call it Indian style. He was floored; purely amazed that he had actually moved them after being motionless for so long.

Spoon still in hand, he found himself scraping the side of the tray, hoping to pick up any small traces of food that might be left behind. Bringing the last small bite to his mouth, he licked the spoon to make sure he had gotten all that he could. Taylor started counting the bricks, which he found himself doing when he was either nervous or bored, in this case, probably both. He started on the wall to his left, systematically counting top to bottom and left to right. One, two, three he counted. His mind fixated on each brick as he counted each individual one staring at it for a moment before moving on. Four, five, six he continued. He jumped to the second row form the top several seconds later. Seven, eight he paused, thinking how much he took his eyesight for granted, He continued saying each number a little louder than the previous. Making sure that his pronunciation was precisely correct; emphasizing twenty, thirty, and forty. Taylor examined every brick for a flaw or slight difference from the rest. Not noticing any irregularities he continued. Forty-one, forty-two, he stopped suddenly. His eyes now focused on the concrete space between brick forty-two and forty-three. He looked closer, squinting his eyes so he did not have to move his body. There was no concrete between the two bricks. That is odd he thought to himself.

Without further hesitation, he started counting again, not wanting to lose his place. Forty-three, forty-four, he continued till reaching forty-eight, forty-nine, and fifty, feeling happy he had reached the top of the next wall he let his thoughts drift off slightly. Thinking about the time his mother would drag him to a boring meeting or a supposedly quick errand turning out to last for hours. Remembering how he would count anything he could see, people, cars, notebooks. Anything to keep him entertained and that would take his mind off the endless boredom. Taylor sighed, thinking to himself "You would think I would learn not to go on errands with her. I guess as a child that thought never crossed my mind. I was probably just happy to get out of the house and go somewhere, thinking it would be more exciting than waiting to play with the friends I didn't really have. Every time I went I only had my hopes of excitement quickly shot down."

"Ten minutes," a muffled voice yelled from beyond the door. Taylor hesitated for a moment, wanting to yell back and get answers to the many questions he had. Controlling his urge to yell back, remembering the welcome his previous questions received the last time he was at the door. Counting a few more bricks he passed brick ninety-four with the small rodent hole located off center at the bottom of the brick just along the floor. The rodents' eyes still not to be seen in the small black hole. He continued counting jumping up to the top of the third wall until he computed the last brick on the third wall. A few moments passed before he pushed his body up onto his knees, his right arm functioning slightly now. He crawled across the room next to the rodent hole so he could count the last wall, the light still perforating through the latch giving him just enough light to finish counting.

He added up faster more excited to reach the end, to achieve this small goal. His eyes were gliding past bricks almost as fast as he could count. One thirty-six, one thirty-seven... he stopped briefly; jumping back to one thirty-six twice as fast as he had gotten there. Staring at the brick, he put his hand flat on the cold floor, pushing his back firmly against the wall behind him and pushing up. His legs felt like he had been doing a wall sit for twenty minutes before he finally reached vertical. With his hands now against the wall holding him in position, Taylor struggled to take a step forward with his right leg. It felt as if he was wearing fishing waiters that had filled up with water. His foot slammed down on the floor forcing a shock wave up his body. Determined to walk forward Taylor focused on his left foot. Only making it a few inches off the ground, just enough to fling his it forward to gain a small amount of distance. One side after another he struggled, slowly moving his way across the floor, until he stood facing some etching on the wall. So intrigued by the markings, he slid his fingers down each notch chiseled in the wall. He had forgotten how excited he was to finish counting the bricks. His fingers pressed into the small notches made by the markings, and slowly he counted the notches, noticing that every fifth one went diagonally across the other four.

"Days," he said to himself. They were counting days. "Thirty-seven," he whispered as if he wanted no one else to hear. His eyes widened staring at the marks. With his fingers still pressed against the notches the latch on the door shut leaving him alone in the dark room once again. Had this person been here for thirty seven days? He stood there in awe. Not knowing what to think. "I do not want to be here for that long. I need to get out." The thought of his family flashed through his mind. He remembered that he dropped his kids off at school, and as he did everything flashed back in an instant. Oh my God! Naucia... Ericka... Jeremy.

Chapter 2

I could hear the nurse walking into the room. Not making a sound until she reached the bed and asked how I was feeling. I gave no response, unaware that she was talking to me. She continued doing the tasks that she had come into the room to do. She took a long look at the screen, monitoring my heart beat, and other vitals, slowly writing them down on the brown clip board, looking at me only occasionally. When she finished she hung the clip board back onto the little hook that was screwed into the desk next to the bed.

She walked to the other side of the bed checking the IV, and the other tubes attached to my body helping me stay alert and alive. After attaching another bag of saline she looked at me, gave me a half a smile, and proceeded toward the door. With the door slightly open I asked in a mumbled voice "What happened?" She looked back with another half smile looking toward the ground non-verbally saying it is not so good. She then stepped outside the door, shutting it quietly behind her. The room was quiet, other than the beeping of my heart rate on the monitor.

My brace prevented me from moving my neck. I shot my eyes horizontally across the room, trying to gain a perspective of what might have gone on, hoping to see my kids, or at least Taylor, wanting to ask them what had happened. Frantically I looked around the room, hoping to find anyone who could give me some information or a word of comfort. Nothing. Slowly shutting my eyes, I replayed the events of the past day, or what I could remember of it; trying to find some answers. I took a few deep breaths trying to relax; thinking it may help.

Feeling a slight chill I remembered pulling the comforter up over my shoulders that morning as I rolled over to see if Taylor had already gotten up to get the kids ready for school, and himself ready for work. I was not expecting him to be cuddling with me like usual, because of the fight we had had the night before; still not exactly sure what it was about. I pulled his unused sheets toward me and curled into a ball on my side of the bed. I looked at the clock sideways trying to focus in on the numbers. As a seven came into focus, I jumped out of bed, knowing that the kids had to be at school at seven thirty. I froze as my feet hit the floor; the blanket now off of me thrown to the other side of the bed half way on the floor.

I shivered as I looked out our bedroom window at the fresh layer of snow that had fallen during the night. I was planning on using that as the excuse to why the kids were late for school. I ran to the kids rooms, but none of them were there. "They never get themselves up" I thought. I remember all the days I heard Jeremy hit the snooze button, forcing me to wake him myself, sometimes being able to choose whatever way I deemed necessary. Scurrying down the stairs, still half asleep, my mouth still having that gross morning taste, I stepped into the kitchen to see the young ones were sitting at the island on their stools peacefully eating their cereal. Jeremy was in the fridge getting food to make the kids sandwiches for lunch. "Where is your father," I asked in a slightly demanding voice. "Outside," said Ericka. Jeremy, jumping into finish her statement, replied "He is warming up the car for us in the garage." "Thank you," I said.

I took a few steps back to glimpse out the window and check if the streets have been plowed. I knew that the snow plows took care of the busier roads first and usually did not get this far up the mountain till later in the afternoon. I saw Taylor outside shoveling the snow from the driveway and sidewalk, about three-fourths done. Gazing at him for a moment, I recalled all the things I loved about him and the happiness we've had together the last twenty five years. A smile came to my face as it does every time I think about him. Remembering the day we took each other's hands and promised to care for one another through the good times and the bad. We gave each other a ring and had that first kiss as partners. It was such a wonderful ceremony, small and intimate, practically perfect.

Taylor and I did not have much money for a ceremony and neither of our families wanted to support our union far less help finance it. They even went as far as to call it a pointless cause. I think back to that day when my grandmother showed up on our doorstep unannounced and extremely unexpected. I stood there in amazement, wondering what she was doing there, when she said, "Well are you going to let me in or not?" I shook my head and swung the door open to welcome her into our home. "What are you doing here?" I remember asking. I got a stern reply, "Well it is your wedding in three weeks, did you really think I would miss it?" In the back of my mind I wanted to say "yes" but didn't have the courage to say it to her face.

"I thought you all disowned me," I said more confused now than ever. "Let me tell you a story," she said as I grabbed her bags from the porch. She quickly proceeded through our home glancing and examining our lives by the items on display. Based on her initial reaction she obviously still flaunted her wealth, and to her we did not compare. "When your grandfather and I announced our engagement, my father went ballistic. He could have killed Tom and not thought anything of it. He hated that man mainly because Tom's father owned an auto mechanic shop

15

on the other side of town and my father always thought that he had been stealing business from his own shop, even though Tom's father would never have done such a thing. When the day of our nuptials arrived my father tried to stop the wedding more than once, the day before the wedding he even went as far as taking me to the next town so I would miss the wedding and keep me from Tom. When he stopped to fill up with gas, I grabbed the door handle as soon as he entered the station to pay and ran. I ran as fast as I could, taking the back roads so my father could not possibly locate me. I ran all night, not stopping for anything. I was so in love, that Tom was all that mattered, not the distance, or my father's disappointment, or even the pain in my body." She explained.

"I finally reached Tom's house. I was afraid to go to mine for the fear that my father would be there, but of course my father, being the smart man that he was, was waiting in the middle of Tom's living room knowing that I would go there. Putting all his anger aside for just a moment, he looked at me and said, "Child, you must truly love this man if you are willing to run all night for him, that, or you're insane. If you are insane, well at least he is nice enough to take you off of my hands. You have my permission to marry Tom, his father and I will try to put our differences aside." He then looked at Tom and said in a stern and demanding voice, "If my daughter is willing to run that far for you, you must not be that bad. But if she ever has to run that far again you better meet her at least half way." Tom smiled at my father nodding his head, still slightly afraid of him. "I will sir," Tom said as he ran over picking me up and kissing me. We then proceeded to get married later that day, to live a long and happy life together."

"What does that have to do with us getting married?" I asked interrupting what I thought was the end of the story. "I'm getting to that part," she replied quite upset that I was rude enough to interrupt her while she was talking. "When I was walking past my fridge and saw your announcement, I thought about all of the horrible things that our family was saying about you and this decision you two have made. It brought my own story back into my mind." She began again, "I thought to myself about how hard it must be for you to have been living on your own since you came out as a teenager. Not knowing where to go or what to do, having no family behind you or anyone supporting you. I realized that you have done all of this on your own, but I'm not going to let you get married without my support."

"Looking back on my engagement, I at least had a mother who supported me up until the end when my father jumped on board with his additional support. I recognized that if you had the strength to do all of this on your own, then you must also really love this man. I did not want you to go through the service thinking no one cared about you, or that no one has felt your struggle. If you are doing this and no one else wants you to, but you can overlook all of that for him, then it truly will last just like your grandfathers and mine did. So, I have come to support you in this decision and meet your fiancé, where is he?" She asked, as she continued walking around the house looking for Taylor.

By this time my eyes were streaming with tears, the idea that someone in my family finally understood how we actually felt was too much. "He is at work and won't be home until later tonight," I said. Her face saddened not realizing what time of day it was. Not caring how emotional this may be and refusing to see me cry, she looked at me and said in a strong voice, "Stop your crying and man up! We have a ceremony to plan." She walked into the dining room placing her designer purse on the table and pulled out a paper and pen. Still standing by the wide open door in awe that she was actually here, I shut it quietly locking it

17

behind me thinking that by doing so I would prevent anyone else from coming. I ran into the dining room where she was sitting, writing lists of things in a notebook. I was still so surprised that she was here.

"Grandma," I said nervous as hell; afraid to say what I was about to say to her. I was quickly interrupted by her reminding me that calling her grandma only aged her. "We have already planned the ceremony." "I know," she replied much more calmly then one might have expected. "But you two do not have enough money to have a nice ceremony," she said judging us from our modest possessions. "If you are anything like me, which I'm sure you are because that is how you were raised to be, then I'm sure you want it to be a lot nicer than what you have planned." "Yes," I said aware that this was a dig at our financial stability. "We did not incorporate all that we wanted to do but we do not have near enough money to do it all," unaware if she knew that or not. "Money is not the issue anymore," she said apparently aware that we did not have much. "I have plenty from your grandfathers passing, and I am sure that he would agree, that we would both want you to have it."

"Wait. What? Why?" I managed to stutter out not knowing what else to say. "Because you two actually love each other and the other grandkids have their parents to help them, and honestly they will probably get divorced anyway. They haven't been through half the shit I'm sure you two have. Hell they can barely make breakfast together without fighting." Apparently she was not a fan of either of my siblings' spouses, or the other cousin's partners I thought to myself, not wanting to know but still slightly curious of the details. "So just tell me everything that you wanted in your first plan and we will start there." She said.

I stood there for a moment in the doorway my grandmother had walked through, staring at Taylor as he walked back toward the garage, before I turned around and headed back toward the kitchen. Our kids were sitting on their stools staring at me as I walked in. "What?" I said in a sarcastic big bully tone as if I would beat them up if they kept looking at me. They kept staring, knowing how I played the game. I bent down in between the girls' chairs and growled in their ears, "Eat your cereal." They kept playing the game knowing that I would keep going because it was the only way I could get them to finish. They were aware of what was coming next and continued to stare at me as I walked away turning around to see if they were still glaring intently at me like they were supposed to.

I ran back to their chairs and swooped both of them up into my arms falling on the floor. I then began tickling them as they would scream and wiggle around pretending like they were trying to escape. "I said eat your cereal." I would yell out teasing them as I continued to tickle their bodies. Eventually letting them over take me and rolling onto my back, letting them tickle me as I would scream and yell for them to get off. Taylor walked into the room during this habitual morning routine. He ran over knowing the game, better than any of us, since he had played the game with his father as a child. He growled as he ran toward us grabbing both of the girls from on top of me and throwing them gently onto the couch.

"We do not tickle Dad." He said, sitting them down. As he cracked a smile, they knew he was joking and jumped into his arms and proceeded to tickle him. Taylor carried them back into the kitchen and placed them back onto the opposite stools that were theirs. Together they yelled out "Daddy." "Oh yeah," he said as he switched them putting them down on their designated seats and giving them both a kiss on the head. "Now eat your cereal before you are late for school," he said. "I don't want to go to school," said Naucia in her sad puppy dog face, or so she always called it, thinking it would get her out of having to go. "You almost done Jeremy?" Taylor said referring to the girl's lunches. Taylor looked up at him waiting for acknowledgement that Jeremy had heard him. "Yeah, they just need juice boxes and they will be all set to go" he replied. "Good. Thank you," Taylor said letting Jeremy know that his efforts were appreciated.

"Lets go girls! Get your coats on. We are going to be late," Taylor yelled out to them. "Taylor," I said as he turned around with the look on his face of what do you have to say now. He probably assumed I was just trying to get the last word in once again from the fight we had last night. "I'm really sorry about last night" I said. "No, it's fine, really" said Taylor, turning back toward the door trying to get the girls out. I could tell that he was still slightly upset from what I had said last night. "No it's not," I said, knowing that I had to fix this and that it was my fault. "You are right," I said almost killing me to have to say it. "I should be more supportive and understanding of your career. I know you have worked hard to get where you are and I would really like to sit down and talk about it again when you get home, ok?" "Ok" he replied unsure if I was actually ready to communicate without fighting. "When I get home we will talk about it but until then do not let the children know what is going on. Please, they will be devastated." "Ok, I won't" I answered him glad that he was agreeing to talk about it again. "Give me a kiss" he said leaning in toward me to whisper in my ear. "I love you and I will see you tonight?" he said kissing me just behind my ear. "Love you" I whispered back as he began to walk back toward the open door. "Goodbye girls" I yelled out to the car, as I leaned against the doorframe with my shoulder. I stood there as I watched the car back out and pull away slowly because of the snow, making tire tracks on the street as they drove away.

I stepped into the kitchen to grab me something to eat before going upstairs to get ready for work. Jeremy looked at me and asked in a concerned voice, having a feeling that he already knew, "What can't you tell us?" "Well I can't tell you, now can I? You heard your father." "Tell me," he said, trying to scare it out of me. "I want and deserve to know what's wrong with dads' career." "Nothing is wrong with his career," I said hoping that I could reassure him. "Well then what is it? I have the right to know" he said. "I know you do, buddy, but your father and I need to discuss it before we make our final decision. At that point we will be more than happy to tell all of you, together. Until then I don't want you to convince me of why I should tell you, OK."

He looked at me afraid to ask the next question, not knowing if he wanted to hear the answer or not. "I heard you guys fighting last night. Is everything going to be ok?" He asked with a cringed look on his face. "Yes," I replied afraid of what he thought was going on. I did not want to make him think anything bad was happening to our family. "It will. We just need to talk it over," I said as I walked toward the fridge to get the milk for my cereal. "I heard dad wants to move," said Jeremy obviously aware of much more than I thought he did. I stopped with the fridge half open, thinking of what to say or how to explain the situation to him without freaking him out. I shut the door, milk in hand. "Jeremy," I said, afraid of his reaction, not knowing if this was happening or not. "Your father, as you know, has been trying to get this position in the company which would enable him to be a lot more flexible with his hours, not to mention a significant pay raise. He really wants to take this position so that he can spend more time at home with you guys and not be forced to be at the office all day like he is now. We would have to move for him to be able to take this position. We were thinking that since the girls just barely started school and you…"

"What?" Jeremy quickly interrupted. "Since I am doing school online, I can do it wherever we happen to go. Did you even think of my friends and Stacy? How am I supposed to see her if we move? Huh, Dad?" He said quite upset. "This is not a for sure thing yet" I said. "Dad," he said interrupting me once again. He was trying to get his point across obviously very upset at this whole situation. "Stacy is the first and only girl that has not run away thinking I'm a freak when I told her that I have two dads and no mom. She is the only one that has actually cared; she actually likes both of you. I'm not going to leave her! I'm not! I'm staying her with her!" he yelled. I tried to stop him but his mind was set as he ran up the stairs furious at me, not realizing that I took his side of the argument last night, when I told Taylor that we should stay.

In a hurry, I grabbed the milk and poured it on my sugar puffs, trying to catch up for lost time; I tilted the bowl toward my mouth and shoveled the puffs in. I tossed the bowl into the sink and ran up the stairs two at a time to get changed. I grabbed the rail post at the top of the stairs and swung myself around the post just as our children did. The feeling of flying came over me as I took only three steps to the corner hearing the sound of my steps echoing off the walls.

I'm sure, the Clements, our next door neighbors heard the sound of my feet against the wood floor. I did not even want to think about what they probably though the sound could be. Thinking of all the times they had called the police on us, only to have the police come to our door and demand to see the kids, because they had a report of child abuse. After the sixth or seventh time of having the Clements call on us, the police finally started to come to our house more casually. They knew that we loved our kids and that we would never hurt them, whether they agreed with the two dads thing or not. We showed them that we had only been playing tag or a game on the TV, which is what was making all of the noise. The cops would take a walk through the house and ask the children questions, only because it was mandatory on a child abuse call. Sometimes they would even sit down at the table and enjoy a hot cup of coffee on extremely cold days. Then they would get down on one knee, at the children's eye level and say, "your fathers love you and if they ever do hurt you, you can come tell us, ok?" "Ok," the girls would say and then yell at the officers as they walked out the door, "Come back and play tea party again soon." Eventually they would giggle and run off into the other room to look out the window as the officers would walk over to the neighbors and finish their report. They kept reminded them that they should not call unless they were certain that we had physically hurt one of the children. Each time the Clements were terribly disappointed that they had been wrong yet again. They were so certain that we hurt our children based off the simple fact that we are gay.

After realizing that the cops could not press charges on us, they decided to call the Department of Child and Family Services. The department would come to our home and threaten to take our children away if they found any proof of us abusing them. We let them know that we would never even think of laying a hand on them. The case worker would sit us down and question us, wondering why our neighbors would call them with probable cause. Taylor always jumped in and answered before I could even open my mouth, "Our neighbors have been causing us problems ever since they found out that we were gay. They have even gone as far as to lure the kids over to their house as they walked home from school." Being old enough to understand Jeremy would grab the girls and run home with them in his arms dropping his backpack on the sidewalk outside their house. When I would go over to their house to get his backpack, they claimed they did not know what I was talking about, and that they would never do such a thing.

I threw off all of my clothes and anxiously waited for the water to come to the right temperature. Frustrated that I would only be there for a few moments, I still did my usual routine, making sure I shampooed and conditioned twice. Grabbing a towel to dry myself off as I stepped out of the shower, I noticed a paper taped on the bathroom vanity. Trying to dry myself, I picked it up wondering what it was. As I opened it, my name was hand written at the top of the page. I continued to unfold it scanning it briefly, and noticed Taylor's name signed at the bottom. My eyes shot back to the top of the page, as I carefully read.

Dear Bryan,

I'm so sorry about last night. I never should have let myself get out of   hand like that. I know you really want to stay here in this neighborhood and I think we should sit down tonight when I get home from work and talk about the pro's and con's. You know that I love you, always have, and always will. I would do anything for you if it would make you happy. Think about it today and what would be the best for us and the kids. I love you honey and I will see you tonight after work.

XOXOXO

Love you,

Taylor

"I love you to," I whispered as I put the paper next to my heart. I stood there for a few moments until the thought of being late for work flooded back into my head. I brushed my teeth, threw some putty into my hair figuring I could style it in the car, and grabbed some clothes in a frantic motion. As I finished putting my second shoe on, I grabbed my suit jacket off the bed and ran back toward the stairs yelling "I love you Jeremy," as I ran passed his room not expecting a reply, today at least, assuming that he was still mad at both Taylor and me. I yanked the keys from the kitchen counter and fetched my briefcase from the table in the office and took off toward the garage. I threw the door to the garage open, and jumped into the car. I pushed in the keys, forced it into reverse and sped down the driveway.

Being so short of time I flew by my usual morning coffee stop, and decided to just drink the nasty coffee at work that Sue makes every morning. I slowly pulled my foot back slightly off the gas, saving energy and pollution, as I coasted down the hill. Seeing the light at the bottom of the street turn green, I continued to coast through the snow. Getting closer to the intersection, the light changed to the always disappointing color of yellow, which meant if you stopped you would be stuck sitting at the light for another sixty seconds or so. I put my foot on the gas and accelerated, hoping to make it through the light before it changed to red. Thinking that the light stayed yellow a little longer than it did I was going too fast to try to stop in the snow anyway. I pushed on the gas as the light changed to red. I glanced quickly both ways. I knew I was running this one, when out of the passenger window I saw a black suburban changing lanes to avoid stopping behind the car in front of him previously stopped at the light, I froze, realizing there was nothing I could do. It was all in God's hands now.

Chapter 3

My eyes shot open as I heard the sound of the two vehicles colliding into one another. The two cars tangled together, smashed into one. I tried to remember more but I couldn't. That was it. The last memory I had. I lay there confused wondering where my family was. The EMT's must have called the In Case Of Emergency number in my phone alerting Taylor of my accident. They should all be here, especially Taylor. My eyes slowly filled with tears, I wanted to wipe them but was unable, to my arms were stuck, numb on the side of my body as if sewn to the hips. My head was the only part I knowingly could move. Even though the neck brace prevented movement to all the corners of the room I knew Taylor and the kids were not there or they would have come to my bed when they had seen me looking around. I looked toward the door seeing someone's face in the small glass window in the hospital door. I was hoping it would be Taylor.

To my dismay it was a very cute female nurse. She had a disgusted look plastered on her face and frantically turned her head away from the window when our eyes met. It was as if she was ashamed to even look at me, or not allowed to. As I lie there looking at the glass window, watching people walk by, I noticed that everyone that looked in, had the same look on their face, making me start to question why. I had enough respect to honor patients' privacy and not look into their room, when I would visit a hospital. Why did they not have the same respect for me, I wondered. After running through a few ideas in my head of why they all had that exact same look on their faces I rested my head back down into my pillow. I was beginning to feel like an animal at the popular zoo by our house. With all the people looking at me, waiting for me to do something more exciting than just lie here, like a trick or planning a jump into the pool. As I rested my head further back into the pillow I began to reminisce back to the wedding.

I sat down at the table looking at my grandma in awe, "Are you serious?" I asked not believing what she had just told me. "Yes!" she replied excitedly. "But the ceremony might be over if you don't hurry up," she quickly chimed in, always being one to throw her little digs in where ever she could. "Ok ok, thank you," I said throwing my arms around her to show her how much it really did mean to me. "I love you. Uh, this is amazing," I said as I kissed her on the forehead. "Ok," I said as she slowly pushed me away politely, having never been a fan of affection. "So our first plan, we wanted to be in a back yard of a huge white house on the grass with bushes, green bushes, all around," I began fantasizing off into my dream. "We wanted it like a vast garden escape, everything fresh and green. The chairs set up on the grass overlooking the vineyard just over the hill and the ocean close off in the distance, not too far beyond the vineyard. Large thin white sheets of cloth hung over the ceremony letting light in to glow about the room beneath, but blocking the direct sun. White wood chairs and a white carpet walkway leading into the backyard and all the way down to the front of the stage that we would be standing on." My grandmother was taking short notes from all my ramblings, not having an abundance of time to write it all down with how fast I was talking.

"We have a few close friends that we want to have as our grooms maids. All of us in black tuxes and white shirts with black bowties. Our friends' two little boys as our flower boys, throwing our white rose petals as they walk down the aisle. Oh and we want it to be a black and white formal ceremony, with all the men in black bowties and the women in black and white dresses. Very formal, we want there to be peacocks walking around the yard giving it all some bright romantic colors." "Ok" she said, interrupting me, seeing that I was only going to ramble on for hours if she did not stop me. "We can do that. I will definitely have to make some calls but we can manage all of that." "Oh my god, I love you grandma," I said as I jumped up and down clapping my hands with the biggest grin on my face like a little school girl telling her friends she had just got asked on her first date. She turned around with a stern look on her face pointing her finger at me, "You better not screw this one up" she said before she turned back around picking up her pen and jotting some more items down. I'm sure throwing some of her own ideas in as well.

As I leaned over her trying to look at the paper to see what she was writing down, her head hung over the paper as if it were a secret. I walked into the hallway grabbing her bags and took them upstairs to the guest room, almost dropping them as I ran in anticipation of what the ceremony was going to look like. After placing the bags on the floor at the foot of the bed, I turned to walk away and saw a picture of Taylor and me on one of our hikes in the redwoods. Beautifully framed up on the wall, I gaze at us looking as happy as ever realizing that this was real and our dreams were coming true, or as true as they could legally be. The sensation of a tear coming to my eyes manifested itself as I shook my head and walked out of the room to our bedroom. I seized the flowers, that Taylor had bought me a few days earlier, from our room and placed them on the dresser in the guest room for my grandmother to enjoy. They were my favorite flowers, because I used to pick them in her garden with her when I was a child, so I knew she would love them as well. I closed the door and pranced back down the stairs. My grandmother was still at the table, writing, with a bottle of red wine open and a half filled glass in her hand.

I grabbed a crystal glass hanging on the side of the wine rack and poured myself a glass, and brought it to my lips allowing the sweet bouquet to flow freely through my palate before taking a sip. We sat there for the next few hours chatting and planning all the details that Taylor and I had discussed in the beginning. We're laughing and enjoying ourselves, catching up on all the family gossip that I had missed over the lost years. As I sat in occasional moments of silence, it began to all sink in. What my grandmother said, comparing us to her and my grandfather was true, and Taylor and I really were going to have a long and happy life together. Looking at her, I had qualms about facing the day when we to would get old and lose the one we loved, passing away and leaving us all alone with nothing to do but wait, like she was doing now.

I jumped up the moment I heard Taylor's car pull into the driveway. I rushed into the garage to tell Taylor the amazing news and all that had happened with my family. As I reached his car door I pulled it open before the car was even stopped, and was about to start telling him the good news when I noticed the sad expression on his face. I stopped, as he stepped out of the car I asked, "What's wrong honey?" The look on his face brought me down from my cloud of happiness. "My mother called yelling at me. She told me that I had embarrassed the whole family by sending those announcements to their neighbors of our ceremony. They all called her in disgust asking her if it was actually true." I quickly wiped the smile off my face, forcing myself not to let it slip back on. "She said that she is so embarrassed that neither she nor any of the family will be attending the ceremony." He said as tears began to well up in his eyes. "She said that I have shamed the family. As she was

29

hanging up the phone she said from this day on, until I change, she no longer considers me her son." "I tried calling her back a few times throughout the day, even from other people's phones at work, but she would never answer knowing it had to be me." I wrapped my arms around him in sympathy hoping that it would help. "It'll be ok babe," I said, not sure it would be, but doing all that I could to try and help, knowing as soon as he got the news of my grandmother it would only make him feel worse. "You know their beliefs, I promise you babe, they'll understand one day," I whispered softly in his ear as I continued to hold him close to me.

As the door closed behind us, I remembered that my grandmother was sitting in our living room and I had not told him the news yet. I did not know if this was the best time or not, but I had realized then that I could not hide it for much longer. Slowing the pace of my footsteps to give me a little more time to explain, I looked at him, but I was unable to start explaining as my grandmother stepped out from around the corner startling both of us. Taylor had a look of surprise and terror on his face not knowing who my grandmother was far less the reason she was in our home. I handed him my glass of wine as she began telling him the same story she had told me. She paused in the middle to introduce herself, realizing that she had not done so yet, then continued, not wanting him to interrupt her story like I did. Taylor's eyes were wide open in amazement at all that was going on, as we all walked into the living room together to sit down and listen to the rest of her story.

Gazing back and forth from Taylor to my grandmother, I spotted a pleasant change coming over his face, as the sadness turned into a grateful smile. My grandmother had finished with her story and had moved on to all of the notes she had written down about our dream ceremony. Finishing the list of things I mentioned, she asked him if there was anything that he would like to add to create our perfectly magical day. Still trying to grasp the whole concept of what we wanted, not being able to think of anything that I had not already mentioned, he shook his head, and responded "No." His comment caused my grandmother to get a surprised look on her face; she was in disbelief that we had already covered all of it. "Ok," she said, in a much excited manner, knowing that she would be getting all the credit for the spectacular event. Taylor looked at me with a face I had never seen on him before. "Bryan," he said. "May I talk to you in the other room for a moment?"

Following him into the kitchen, he stared at me blindly, not knowing where to start. "Why didn't you tell me about this before?" "I didn't know about it until today, when she showed up on our doorstep, telling me the same story she just told you. I had absolutely no clue she was going to do this, or even come to the ceremony at all," I said, obviously just as stunned as he was. By the look on his face, I realized what my own face must have looked like earlier today, when I first saw her. "Is she serious about all this?" He asked. "Yeah she is," I replied shaking my head in disbelief. "I know it's crazy but she wants to do this for us and you know that we both would much rather have this then the other ceremony we were planning on, and now we have the money to do it." He shrugged his shoulders, before stepping forward putting his hands in mine and kissing me. "Oh and she is staying in the guest room," I tossed in as we were walking back to the living room, knowing it would prevent him from backing down and saying no, if he knew she could hear. He agreed, with a frustrated look, and began chatting with my grandmother about the ceremony and what I was like as a child, as I went back into the kitchen to start preparing dinner.

I grabbed the chicken out of the fridge, pulled a pot off the hook hanging above the granite island in the middle of the kitchen, and filled it with water. I tossed in the pasta when the water was at a rapid boil and put the chicken in the pan to sauté. Today I didn't listen to the radio while I was cooking but instead I listened to my fiancé and my grandma talk in the other room, happy that they were getting along so well. As I was preparing the alfredo sauce my grandmother and Taylor both walked in startling me slightly.

My grandmother sat there with her notebook in front of her on the counter, keeping one eye on me, looking for ways to critique me on my cooking skills, or the lack thereof. Considering she is and always will be the master chef in the family; having no one tell her otherwise. Taylor walked around the island, kissing me on the cheek as he passed by, grabbing the plates form the wood cabinet and the utensils from the drawer to help set the table. After placing the plates and utensils on the table, he headed back into the other room to bring the half bottle of wine, and the glasses to the table, grabbing an extra glass for himself. Placing the wine on the table and finishing off with the cloth napkins, he resumed his position, talking to his soon to be grandmother in-law in our minds, about the big day. I listened to them chat back and forth, amazed that this was all really happening and not just some wonderful dream. I finished putting the final touches and spices on the chicken alfredo and walked it to the table before announcing that dinner was ready. They hurried over, washing their hands in the sink before joining me at the table. All of us starving and excited about the days ahead and the one big day to come.

Turning to Taylor, I asked him to say a blessing on the food, knowing that my grandmother was a very religious woman, and would not have the food go unblessed. As we all sat there enveloped in the happiness of the day and enjoying the meal I had prepared, my grandmother looked at both of us and with a puzzled look said, "I have a question." We both looked at each other, before looking at her, intrigued at what she may want to know. Giving her our attention, she started. "Looking at both of you I see that you are both pretty masculine guys, so that makes me wonder which one of you is the woman in the relationship?" She asked, thinking it would be an awkward question for us, unaware that it is actually a very common question people ask. We looked at each other holding back our laughter because of the many times we have been asked that question. Then looking back at her we gave her the same answer that we gave to everyone else that asks. "Neither of us plays the role of a woman in the relationship. We are both males, and play the role of male. We both go to work every day and come home. We take turns cooking and doing all the other chores around the house. We really do not take parts in this relationship. We are just two men who happen to like men."

She looked at us in a slightly confused manner, not really understanding how that would work, but trying to work it out in her head. "Any other questions?" I asked, knowing that she was a very blunt old woman and may go as far as to ask the second question everyone else asks, of "Who the pitcher is and who is the catcher," or something along those lines, possibly slightly more refined. Surprisingly she responded with a "No," probably not being able to build up enough courage to ask, which coming from her was very surprising. Taylor and I held hands firmly under the table, using the other hand to scrap the last remaining sauce off of our plates. Finishing about the same time, we relaxed giving grandma and extra minute or two, before I began to clear the table. Without hesitation my grandmother stood up, slapping my hand that was reaching out for her plate, saying "You cooked. Taylor and I will clean up. We have a few more things we still have to discuss." She claimed looking at Taylor to let him know that he did not have a choice in the matter. He nodded back acknowledging his willingness to do what she suggested.

He rose removing the utensils from my plate. He added them to his and placed them on my grandmothers' plate, then stacked them and proceeded toward the kitchen. "Thank you," I shouted making sure he could hear me from the kitchen. "No, thank you babe," his reply came shortly after from the far side of the kitchen. He made his entrance back into the room giving me a kiss on the head then looked toward my grandmother and thanked her as well, realizing that she had conned him into this and she did not have any intention on helping. But neither Taylor nor I minded, knowing that she had already done far too much. I nodded in agreement letting her know the gratitude that we both had for her. Granting me a smile in return, they continued their business in the kitchen as I proceeded toward my bedroom, for a little time to take it all in. Stopping about half way up the stairs, I gazed at the pictures of Taylor and me hanging on the wall, realizing how many times I have just run past them without acknowledging their existence. But tonight I stopped to look at each one of them until reaching the second picture from the top that stopped me in my tracks.

My eyes fixated on the picture. I just stood there for a few moments before reaching forward and removing the picture form the wall. I sat on the stairs, as my eyes started to swell up with tears. I reminisced back to the mountain retreat that Taylor and I had gone on a year or so ago when this picture was taken. Sitting by the fire in the lounge of the log cabin, looking out the window at the snow covered mountains and the contrasting dark green pine trees scattered about. Laughing contently in each other's company, sitting on the leather chair together our feet propped up on the ottoman and listening to each other's stories about our most embarrassing moments. Laughing and enjoying ourselves, leaving all our problems at home. My eyes still on the picture, I remembered the faces of the cute couple that came up to us later that day while we were relaxing in the hot tub watching the snow fall down on us from the frosty night sky. They asked us how we were doing, as they jumped into the hot tub to join us, introducing themselves as Ben and Alex. "Good," we replied introducing ourselves and asking the routine introductory hot tub questions that you would ask someone when you are on vacation. After getting through the customary introductions and waiting for the awkward silence to set in, they both looked at each other and then back at us blurting out a comment as if it was a race to see who could do it the fastest. They both laughed, realizing that we could not understand a word either of them had just said. Ben then restarted what they both had tried to mutter. "Earlier today when you two were sitting in the lounge looking out the window we were watching you. We were amazed at how much you two were enjoying yourselves. We sat back watching in admiration until Alex took out our camera and snapped a shot of you two. It really is the cutest picture that I have ever seen in my entire life. If you would like us to email a copy of it to you, we would be more than happy to so you two can remember this fantastic vacation." "Yeah we would like that," said Taylor. "Thank you," I added in agreement.

Drying the tears on my face and wiping the tear spots on the glass that covered the picture, I placed the photo back to its original spot on the wall. I knew that this was the picture I wanted on the welcome table next to the guest book at the ceremony. In a few weeks I will have the best day of my life and I couldn't keep the smile off my face thinking about it and how wonderful it will be. Walking into my bedroom, thoughts of the ceremony ran through my head. I thought of all our friends that would be there dinning and enjoying a romantic night with us.

After planning a few more details about our special day, Taylor said goodnight to my grandmother and retired to our room to join me in bed. As he entered the room, he had the biggest grin on his face that I had ever seen. He took a few steps forward pouncing over the footboard landing on the bed beside me, not wiping that smirk off his face for even one moment. We both laid there staring at each other, giddy as could be, knowing that this was the beginning of the rest of our lives. He removed his clothes and joined me under the sheets. Although my grandmother stayed downstairs for a short while longer finishing up some ideas of her own, I'm sure she could still hear us from there, professing our love and excitement sexually to one another, before rolling over and holding each other in love, gratitude, excitement, and joy as we both drifted off to sleep.

Our eyes shot open as the alarm clock went off. Smacking the snooze button I rolled over to look at Taylor, knowing that today was the day that we would be partners for the rest of our lives. I looked at him for a moment, before jumping out of bed ecstatic about the events of the day, then running down the stairs to start breakfast for us all. I placed one foot onto the kitchen floor and stopped in my tracks, the food was already set out on the counter. "About time you two lazy heads got up," said my grandma as she turned the corner and walked into the kitchen, unaware that we had already been up for a while. "How long have you been up?" I asked, feeling even lazier after asking. "Long enough to make sure everything goes flawlessly today," she said trying to make us realize that if we screw any part of this day up she would never let us live it down.

"The breakfast looks delicious, thank you" said Taylor as we started eating. "Grandma," I said before stopping myself not wanting to get yelled at for aging her once again. "I just wanted to thank you again for all that you have done for us these last few weeks. We really do appreciate it, more than we could ever express. Your efforts in making this the dream ceremony we wanted makes it feel that much more like a real wedding." "I know," she replied. Understanding how we felt, as well enjoying the power that came from being totally in charge of everything. The day continued to go off without a hitch, thanks to my grandmother and her loyal support. There was only one thing I would have changed about the whole day and that is to have Taylor's family and my own family there to share in our happiness. The only memory I have of them that day was a letter I received telling me how disappointed they were in me and that they never wanted to see or talk to me again. The letter also stated that they find my lifestyle disgusting and the ceremony total nonsense. They laughed at the idea of two men being in love, and joked about me choosing to be gay.

As I lie in the hospital bed, a tear rolled down my cold face remembering all of our friends who were there to support us and congratulate us that day. Moments later my smile faded from my face, as I remembered my grandmothers horrible passing only a few months later, and how our ceremony was her last great accomplishment. I wished my family would have told me about her passing, before I saw it in the online obituaries, finding out too late to attend the funeral service, but knowing that my family did not tell me because they truly did not want me there. I glanced at my reflection in the TV that hung from the ceiling in front of me, collecting enough energy to lift my arm just high enough to press the little red button on the side of the bed to alert the nurse's desk that I needed them. A few moments later a different nurse, but with the same expression of disgust and empathy on her face, came into the room shutting the door behind her and approached my hospital bed. In a voice that sounded pretentious like a child saying they're sorry but not really meaning it, she asked "What may I do for you?" At the same time leaning over to reset the flashing call light. "Could you turn on the TV and open the blinds for me please?" I asked in a raspy voice, my throat still dry from the lack of fluids. She turned walking toward the window without a word, completing the tasks I asked her to do. As she turned the blinds upward rays of sunlight splashed to all corners of the room. Turning back, she grabbed the remote from the nightstand and flipped on the TV. "What do you want to watch?" She said in a slightly less annoyed voice. "I don't know. What's on?" I replied, as she flipped through the channels starting at the higher double digit numbers pausing on each channel for a few moments before continuing down the line in search for something that was pleasing to me.

Reaching the single digit numbers, she paused a little longer on each channel, hoping I would find something soon so that she did not have to start back again at the top. Realizing that the next channel she flipped to was one of my favorite day time talk shows, I grunted in approval letting her know I wanted her to keep it there. Placing the remote next to my hand, she asked, "Anything else I can do" her eyes meeting mine. "Yes," I said in a very slow but mild tone. "Why is everyone looking into my door window?" She gave me the same half smile the first nurse had given me, biting her lip to keep from saying what she really wanted to say and headed toward the door.

"Ma'am, please" I yelled out in desperation as she turned around and saw the tears flowing freely from my eyes. She looked at me with an expression of concern, she swallowed her saliva in a nervous fashion and said, "I can't tell you," giving me the look of, I wish you knew but I don't want to be the one to have to tell you. She turned toward the door again, refusing to acknowledge my need of knowing. I knew something was terribly wrong, I assumed that it had to be something with Taylor since he was not next to my hospital bed. "What has happened to my husband?" I asked, demanding to be told, as tears still flowed from my eyes, like a steep canyon creek after an abrupt desert rain shower.

Frustrated that I kept persisting, she stomped back toward my bed, placed her hands on the side bars of my bed, and yelled in a hushed voice. "I cannot tell you anything that happens in this hospital. Not about your husband, not about the people that keep looking into your room, not about the patient in the next room, hell I can't even tell you some of the things that pertain to your own health. The patient confidentiality act prevents me as a nurse from telling you anything that happens in this hospital. So don't keep asking us to tell you because we can't." She stormed back toward the door knowing it would be her last time. Her anger rubbing off on me. Her hand reached out for the door as the anger in me, and the need to know what happened grew. I cocked my head toward her, not realizing what I was about to say would hit straight into her heart and in a desperate bold voice I said, "Can't or won't?"

Chapter 4

    Taylor slid his finger down the last ray of hope from the man's life engraved on the wall, as he wondered what that man's last day here must have felt like before he collapsed onto the cement floor. His head resting in the palms of his hands in total disbelief that he was even here. The small amount of light still permeated through the window above him. Taylor's eyes ricocheted around the room in hopes of finding a way to get out of here. His eyes shot back and forth frantically as he remembered the two bricks at the bottom of the first wall that were missing cement between them. Picking himself up off of the dirty floor, he dragged his half lifeless body over to the wall and laid down next to it. Extending his arm out, and pulling out a few rocks that had been forced in the cracks between the bricks in order to make a somewhat tight seal.

    After removing the last rock wedged in the crack, he blew, right into the center clearing away the dust in order to peak all the way through. Glaring through the opening to the equally dim room on the other side, Taylor watched for movement of any kind. He knew there must be someone there because the rude man giving out food stopped outside his door just as he had his. All he could see were bricks on the other side of the room, but determined to know who was over there; he brought his mouth to the hole and whispered into it hoping someone would hear him. "Hello," he whispered, bringing his eyes quickly back to the hole, to see if anyone was looking back at him. Dissatisfied with the results he repeated his greeting again in a slightly louder voice. "Hello." This time he kept his eye in the hole the whole time, fixed upon catching a glimpse of a person, any person.

Not seeing anyone or hearing anything in response to his greetings, Taylor grabbed one of the smaller rocks from between the bricks, stuck it on his thumb in front of his pointer finger and flicked it through the hole and into the next room. Before hearing the sound of the rock skip off the floor, a man's eye emerged in front of the hole. It obstructed most of the light from reaching the sides of the crack. "Hello," Taylor whispered again, hoping for a polite response. "What?" The man said in a bothered tone. "Hi," Taylor said pausing briefly not expecting that particular response from him, before continuing on with his inquiry, "What am I doing here?" The man chuckled in response, Taylor did not understand what could possibly be funny. "I get that a lot," the man replied after he finished his laugh.

"I will give you credit for being the fastest person so far to uncover the hole and ask me that question." "Thank you," Taylor answered in a very confused voice not knowing what else to say to that remark. The man continued chuckling in a deep, old smooth voice before adding "I have been in this jail cell for many, many years, which frankly I probably deserve. I have seen a lot of people come in and out of here. Some stay here awhile and some only a few days before either committing suicide or being moved to another cell to live out their lives." Taylor's body cringed at the thought of someone committing suicide in his cell, and as he remembered back to his wretched childhood when he too had tried to commit suicide. "I've gotten pretty used to the whole situation after I came to the conclusion that the world was better off having me in here and not out there with other people. Not to mention better for me. A lot less stressful in here," he said as he moved slightly, letting some light in so he could see me a little better.

41

His remark reconfirmed to Taylor that he was definitely in jail, even though he was still not sure what he had done to get there. The man continued not caring if Taylor was listening or not, "The last forty years have not been that bad though. After being in here that long, the guards have lightened up a little and slip me a book or magazine every now and then. The thing that saddens me the most about all of this is that my family never comes to visit me, not once. I mean I know I did some bad things but everyone makes mistakes, some are just bigger than others. You have to learn to pick yourself back up and get on with your life, you know?" He said waiting for a response, happy to have someone new to talk to. "I know exactly how that is," Taylor said actually knowing exactly what the man meant.

"My whole family stopped talking to me, they wouldn't even respond to my letters or phone calls," Taylor said. "I used to hope that maybe on my birthday or around the holidays, Christmas especially, they would try to contact me. But after a few years of getting my hopes up, only to be horribly disappointed, I stopped hoping. I figured they were never going to come around and accept me, or even try to understand," Taylor explained. "What did you do that made them hate you so much?" The man inquired. Taylor chuckled slightly under his breath before answering the man, "I accepted who I was put here on earth to be, and started to live my life the way I knew that I was supposed to be living it. All the while my whole family and my religion shunned me and said I was following the devil. I lied to my family, to my church, and more importantly to myself for nineteen years of my life. Until one day I built up enough courage to face it all. To tell my parents, the truth of who I was, and what I wanted to do, and what I was supposed to do with my life."

"We were sitting at the dinner table, all of my brothers and sisters were there. They kept giving me an awkward look like they knew something was up. I think my sister knew exactly what I was going to say, she glared at me with a cold disappointed look that I had never seen on her face before. About half way through dinner I looked up, my eyes meeting with my mothers, and I said "I have something to say." Knowing this was going to be good, my sister's head shot up waiting for the look of shock to come on our mother's face. My sister was eager to jump in and comfort her, waiting for the golden opportunity to replace me as mom's favorite child. Taking a quick survey of everyone at the table before directing my eyes back on my mother, I began to explain that I had not been truly honest with them, and what I was about to say may come as a shock to many of them. I knew it wouldn't be to my sister, who was still on the edge of her seat waiting to rush into our mother's arms to comfort her.

I stumbled awkwardly around the subject, trying to delay my message. But eventually took a deep breath and spit it out. "I'm gay," I said loud enough that they would all hear so I would not have to repeat myself. The whole family gasped. Their eyes wide open filling with tears. My sister ran over to my mother, trying to calm her, hoping she was moving into that favorite spot. My father looked at me with distain, confusion, and anger. He immediately began to diminish my choices telling me how wrong it was and that it did not fit into Gods' plan. He told me I was never to tell anyone again or it would shame the family name. I tried explaining my feelings for an hour, although it felt like an eternity, until I retreated to my room, knowing it was hopeless, they would never understand. Not because they couldn't but simply because they did not want to try. After a few days I left home and stayed at my friends place for three weeks before meeting a few other gay men that also needed a place to stay. Together we rented a duplex and tried to make the best of it.

Different boys came and went over time, finally there ended up being three of us in the house. We became great friends throughout the whole journey. I will never forget the great times we had together, the birthdays, the holidays; we grew so close as we became each other's family and support system. We would cry together and laugh together, we always treated everyone that came into our home as family because that's what we were, family, and for some of us like myself, it was the only family we had. I eventually moved out when I found Bryan the man I wanted to live the rest of my life with.

Bryan and I found a cute little home and started there until we could afford to move into a nice house up on the hill, overlooking the city, with a beautiful tree lined street, and a great neighborhood for us and our children to grow up in." Taylor lifted his head off the ground to look back at the man on the other side of the wall. He had a somewhat disgusted look on his face but at the same time tears were falling. Taylor could see in his face that he had just broken a few stereotypes that that man must have had in his mind about gays and the way they conducted their lives. He looked at Taylor not knowing what to say. He obviously did not meet many gay people in this cell, or at least ones that would admit it. Trying to change the conversation a little he proceeded to ask Taylor what he was in for, and why he was here. "I don't actually know," Taylor replied. Contemplating upon what he could have possibly done that could have caused him to end up here.

"I overheard the guards saying something about you beating up an old woman or something at the hospital," he said. As soon as he mentioned the hospital, Taylor's mind was overwhelmed by emotions, as the incident came flashing back to him. He remembered every little detail, every little noise. Speaking as fast as he could, he told the man what he had done that had brought him here. Taylor was surprised by what actions he had taken, knowing he would have only done it for the man he loved. "Wow!" The man replied in astonishment. "You did all that for a man?" Bothered that the man would say such a thing, I calmed myself by thinking that he apparently did not understanding the meaning of love. Taylor snapped back "Not just a man. He is my husband of over twenty five years. I love him more than anything or anyone else I have ever known and I would do anything for him, anything." Taylor sat there shocked and surprised at his actions but yet somewhat proud of what he had done. He had always been that type of man to act instinctively without thinking so he was not surprised. He knew it was wrong but acknowledging at the same time that what he did was somewhat right.

***

Not expecting her to, the nurse paused, taking what I had said to heart. My face was covered in tears once more. The tears meeting at my chin like two rivers merging into one. She stood there listening to my cry for help, for knowledge, for comfort, and for truth. Knowing that she knew what I needed to hear at that precise moment. Torn between the law and her ethics as a human being she tried to put herself in my situation, to understand how I felt. Then turning abruptly, her eyes welling with tears, she looked at me confused at all the emotion. Knowing how frantic I felt, she looked as if she may collapsed to her knees, her head bowed down unable to look at me. Her anger toward me tossed aside and replaced by understanding and eagerness to help.

Both of our eyes flowed freely with tears, both for very different reasons. My heart pounded in sync with the beat of her footsteps hitting the floor with a determined thud echoing throughout the room. Reaching over my half limp body, she placed her hands gently on top of mine holding them firmly for a moment. Then reclaiming her grip, she grabbed at her scrubs to wipe off the excess tears. Before placing her palm back on top of my cold hands, all the while keeping eye contact, she took a deep breath, cleared her throat, inhaled and in a very quiet and respectful manner and said "I have never understood, nor tried to understand, how you gay people felt towards one another, how you possibly love someone of the same sex. I just could not imagine it and still don't, but the look I see on your face, the look of caring and concern, the look of love toward your partner. You two obviously share the same love that I have toward my husband and kids. When I put myself in your situation and imagined myself in this hospital bed, having no clue where my children or husband were and having everyone refuse to provide me with that highly needed confirmation, I feel sorry for you. I feel your pain. I'm honestly not sure why I turned around because this is just my job, but something inside told me to. I want to help you because I would want someone to help me if I was in your position." She said. I could tell that something inside of her was fighting and forcing her to stay. "Taylor should have been allowed up here." She said making me wonder what had happened. She probably didn't know our rights but I would like to think that she would agree that just because the state will not let us get married, we should still have the same rights as other American citizen, not only because that is what's right, but also because that is what America is all about, justice for all.

She chuckled to herself for a few moments before continuing. "I'm a poor African black woman, so I know how it feels to be kicked out. To have other people try to push you around, telling you that you are of second class status and I will be the first to say that just isn't right." Chuckling a little more, I nodded my head in agreement. Her humor slowly made my smile reappear. With her hands still pressed down against mine, she leaned closer toward me, her serious facial expressions quickly returned. In hopes that it might ease the pain I was feeling and fill the need of knowing, she lowered her voice, to explain to me what had happened only a few hours ago. "This morning about ten o'clock, I happened to be downstairs at the front desk collecting some medical files for some of our patients. Your husband came running into the emergency room entrance throwing the double doors open and with a frantic look on his face, pounded his hands firmly on the top of the counter at the front desk demanding that the clerk tell him what had happened to you and where you were.

A nurse nearby tried to get control of the matter by attempting to calm him by asking in a soothing voice what your name was and how he was related. He quickly replied with your name and that he was your husband. As soon as your husband had mentioned that, the old nurse's head shot up with a nasty little look of joy on her face, rudely asking if your marriage was recognized by the state, knowing full well it was not. Your husband looked at her in disgust, replying with a discouraging, "No." The smile on the face of that old bitch grew. She was obviously firmly against gay rights and you people in general. She looked down her nose at your husband, her next words, meant to sting like a bee, saying, "Then you cannot see him until one of his immediate family members arrives to admit you." "He has not talked to any member of his family for over twenty years. We have no clue if they even exist," your husband replied letting her know the situation. "Shouldn't have chosen to be gay then," she mumbled under her breath as she began to turn around to continue filing papers.

Your husband then proceeded to grab her, pulling her back toward him obviously very ticked by her last comment. Her chest was over the counter, with his hands holding her clothing at the shoulders, her feet a few inches off the floor. He reached forward snatching the scissors in the cup full of beans and pens from behind the desk. He shoved them up toward her neck in a rage of anger. The ward clerk carefully picked up the phone and dialed 911 not wanting your husband to see her. Your husband looked at the old nurse in the eyes and said, "We have been married for over eighteen years, and have been together for twenty five, so you better let me know where my husband is right this second." She stared back with fear in her eyes and answered, "I'm sorry but I cannot legally let you know any information about him. Please feel free to sit in the lobby and wait." She managed to get that out before he threw her back over the desk where she fell to the ground holding her neck, relieved to be free of his tight grip. Your husband paced back and forth before placing his head against one of the cement pillars in the hallway in distress not knowing what to do.

Sobbing uncontrollably, he walked back toward the front desk and apologized to the old nurse asking if she was okay. She would only look up with a scowl toward your husband. All the while we just sat there in shock by the whole event that took place before us. Your husband even bent down onto one knee to beg for her forgiveness and asked where you were again as she continued to scowl at him and refused his plea." As she said that I shook my head. Knowing Taylor all too well and knowing how hard it was for him to ask forgiveness, I knew how sincere he must have been. "When she caught a glimpse of the cops coming down the hall she let out a piercing scream, to gain their attention and make your husband look even worse than he already did. Grabbing your husband and tossing him aside, they quickly began asking her if she was ok.

She yelled back at them in a fake terrified cry, "That man

tried to kill me." She pointed toward your husband as he stood up trying to explain to them what had happened, his words falling on deaf ears. He became more and more frustrated. He thought that the cops, out of anyone, would listen to his case and help him locate you or at least get information about your condition. But instead of coming to his aid, they yelled pointing their guns at him and demanded that he get on the floor. Determined to explain this situation and get help in finding you he did not obey their order to get on the floor and instead turned to face them.

One of the officers reached into his equipment belt, pulled out his taser and shot it at your husband. He immediately went limp, falling to the floor like a cracked egg. He did not move after that. It must have totally stunned him, because he was lifeless as they drug him out the doors and placed him in the backseat of the police car and drove off. Two officers stayed behind to make sure the old nurse was okay and to file a report. They got a statement from the old nurse and our version's of the story. I was one of them that had to fill out a witness sheet. Now I wish I would have been less judgmental toward your husband and stood up for him.

"I'm sorry I did not defend your partner." She said, her eyes beginning to water again. I raised my hand slowly to her face and wiped the tears from her eyes. I looked at her and replied in a soft forgiving voice, "It's okay, and although he is not my husband legally I would appreciate you referring to him as such because to me that's what he is." Holding my tears back I forced myself to stutter out the next few words knowing the answer would not be good. "What happened to him?" Her lips trembled for a moment before replying "I don't know…jail I assume."

Chapter 5

I had to get up. I had to get out. I could not lie here with my husband out there, as far as I knew in jail. Reaching for the edge of the bed I lifted myself up, I swung my feet over the side, the nurse was reaching for the door when she turned back, in time to catch me as I fell slowly to the floor. I was grateful she was a big woman to help break the fall as I landed in her arms. Rolling over and helping me to a standing position, she yelled "What the hell do you think you're doing." I looked at her with a very stern look, and replied with a sincere but determined attitude, "I'm going to find him. If he is in jail, I am going to get him out and let him know I'm okay. When he gets stressed or in uncomfortable situations he acts very impulsively. I promise you it's better for all of us if I find him. She looked at me knowing there was nothing she could do to stop me, and anything she tried to do would only make things more difficult for me, but in no way prevent me from reaching him.

Looking at me in disapproval, but understanding my feelings, she shook her head and said, "Stay here for just a second and I promise I will not try to stop you. Just wait here, I will only be a moment, OK" Not knowing where she was going or what she was doing, I debated if I should leave in fear that she would bring security back, or trust her and wait. I needed to make my decision quickly. She would be back any minute. Looking around the room, still holding firmly to the bars on the bed, I let go. I balanced myself briefly at the side of my bed, testing the strength in my legs. I took a step forward with my right foot, surprised that it moved, since I didn't have sensation in either of them. Slowly I moved one foot in front of the other as if I was a baby learning how to walk for the very first time. I understood that I needed to speed things up if I was to make it out of here before she returned. I took a few more steps toward the door, grabbed the handle and pushed it down. The door swung open towards me, almost knocking me off balance. I proceeded into the hall, pausing for a moment to see if the nurse was anywhere in sight. Not seeing her I shuffled as fast as I could, gripping tightly onto the old dirty wood rails attached to the hospital walls.

Thinking that the nurse went to get the guards, and not wanting to take the risks of running into them in the elevator, I opted to take the stairs instead. I worried that if I was caught, they would take me back to my room and force me to stay there. Holding tightly to the rail, I cautiously took the stairs one at a time. I knew at any moment my legs could give out causing me to fall down the stairs, so I put all my weight onto my hands and arms. My heart longing to see Taylor once again, as I made my way down the stairs, I was not able to recall any other time that I had ever wanted to see him more than I did right now.

I felt my heart moving downward into my stomach faster than I was moving down the stairwell. Just the thought of being in his position was terrifying. Not knowing if I was dead or alive. Not being able to find out due to a bias law. As I recalled the story the nurse had told me about what Taylor had done, I put myself in his shoes. I realized that I probably would have done the same thing knowing I would be that enraged as the political man that I am, with my emotions out of control. But at the same time I would hope I would be able to handle it slightly better, after all Taylor freaks unnecessarily when placed in situations like this. I can usually stay calm and think logically, I thought. I was surprised that my legs had made it down the stairs at all, still holding firmly to the rail, my excitement grew when I reached the last two stairs. With my hand already outstretched for the door in order to save as much time as possible, I swung the door open towards me and stepped into the hallway. I pushed myself further down the hallway, grabbing onto the discolored wood rails whenever available, trying to save as much energy as possible. My legs began giving out and my knees buckled after every few steps as I continued to push myself down the hall. The rotating glass exit doors were now in sight. I turned my face toward the wall as I walked past the front desk; I knew if they saw me they would stop me from leaving. Reaching the revolving doors, I pressed my hands up on the glass and followed it around to the outside.

I inhaled the frozen air deeply, through my nostrils and into my lungs, before exhaling it in a cloud of fog forming in front of my face before it disappeared into the cold white sky. As I slowly walked down the entrance toward the sidewalk, I could feel the snow crunching beneath my bare feet. I must hurry and find him, I thought. Struggling to regain focus, I lifted my head up, my arms out to my side helping with my balance on the slippery sidewalk.

At the end of the roundabout of cars dropping off patients to the hospital, I turned and walked towards the main street where I could grab a cab. As I did, I was hit in the shoulder with a packed ball of snow. "I told you to stay in your room till I came back. Not to come walking out here with only a gown on. You are going to freeze your nuts off." Squinting my eyes to block out the reflection of the light off the snow I noticed my black nurse standing behind a rusted purple station wagon. She had a disappointed kind of look on her face as she ran over to help me to her car. Squeezing my side, she muttered under her breath, "What the hell were you thinking?" Helping place me down into the seat of the car she slammed the door behind me and ran around to get behind the wheel.

I began kicking empty fast food bags aside to make room for my feet, and reached behind to grab the seat belt, only to realize that there was not one for this seat. Since I had already almost died once today it did not seem like such a big deal. Staring at her for a moment, as we pulled away from the curb, I anxiously ask, "What are we doing?" "We're going to find your husband," she replied, surprising me with that answer. I was glad that she began referring to him as my husband. "What?" I answered confused by her response and still in disbelief. "Why are you helping me?" I asked still looking at her face, her eyes glued to the road. A few moments passed before her lips began to move. "Just let me do this, ok?" She said, not yet exactly sure why she was doing this just feeling that she should. I nodded my head in agreement. "Put these on," she said as she reached in the back seat, grabbing some of what I assumed were her husband's clothes, before tossing them onto my lap, implying that I should do it now.

I began pulling the pants up under the hospital gown, slowly unbuttoning them. Before grabbing the shirt thrown across my lap and putting it on, I realized that this man was definitely a much bigger man then myself. I put the rest of the clothes on as she continued to talk. "I'm sure the police took him to jail. We'll start there." Knowing that at this point she knew more than I did, I trusted her judgment. We began to pass by cars at a much faster pace than I would have thought this car could go, but glad it did. Not knowing exactly where we were, I began to look for road signs to help me determine our location. Searching the side of the road for a few miles we eventually passed a road sign with a big black 106 printed on it, meaning nothing to me.

Removing her hand from the wheel, she began fidgeting with the stereo, the signal was fading in and out. I was not expecting much more than that from the look of this car. Looking down the dashboard, I noticed the clock reading 2:53. My eyes bulged. "Is that the correct time?" I yelled, startling her a little. "Yes, yes it's correct. What do you think I drive, a broken car?" She replied, giving me no time to comment on the remark. I grabbed the wheel yanking it to one side, yelling for her to exit and pointing to the off ramp. Pulling across a few lanes of traffic and cutting off a car we managed to get to the off ramp before she turned and slapped me and yelled "What are you thinking?" "My kids!" I yelled back at her, not realizing that it honestly meant nothing to her because she was unaware that I even had kids. "My son has a game today, so he can't pick up Naucia and Ericka from school like he usually does. I was supposed to pick them up," I responded. "Won't some other parent drive them home?" She asked in a rude tone.

"No," I yelled back at her in a very stern voice. "All the other parents think they are satanic because Taylor and I are gay. Our neighbors, the Clements, always try to wait at their school, pretending to be their grandparents', trying daily to pick them up before we can so they can take them to Division of Child and Family Services and get them taken away." "What? Why would they do that?" She asked confused by the whole situation. "Doesn't the school do anything about it?" "No. The principal is on their side and will not do anything about it," I replied, getting ready to pull a picture of them out of wallet, before remembering that I was not in my own clothes. "How many kids do you have?" She asked. "Just the three," I replied before I was interrupted. "They from a previous wife or something?" She asked thinking that was the only way a gay couple could have any children. "No," I answered with a disgusted look on my face from the thought of marrying a woman, far less procreating with one. "We adopted the girls from Africa and Jeremy from Romania," I managed to say before being interrupted once again by her.

"What?" She yelled at the windshield as my head was thrust back into the headrest as we sped down the road, obviously very motivated to save the African kids. I was slightly scared for my life at the way she was driving, looking back at the clock now reading 2:55. "Shit," I said, realizing that we were running out of time and still many blocks away from the school. "We have five minutes before school lets out." Jumping back on the freeway, we headed back the way we had just come. I directed her as we went, telling her about my kids and answering all the questions she had for me about adopting them. I explained to her that it was a lot harder for Taylor and me to adopt than it was for a straight couple in America. She sat there very interested, with a curious look on her face. She was obviously thinking very deeply about something and trying to get to the bottom of it. "When we went over to Africa, for the first time, to get our oldest daughter we saw all the famine and death going on at that time. It made us want to take the entire population of children home with us. We knew that was unrealistic. We just had to do what we could at that time."

The look on her face was as if she was deep in thought. "As we were walking through one of many orphanages', we came across this little girl. Our eyes met with hers. While standing there staring at her we knew she was the one. They had told us that their father had just died from malaria and that they had no mother or any other family. Leading us to the question of who was the they? Only to be informed that she had an older sister whom we ended adopting as well, not wanting to split up what family they had left. The African people were more than happy to let us adopt her, but it was the American government that was presenting a problem. Taylor and I, being gay, made it much more difficult for the government to let us adopt them. The government made us jump through hoops that no one else had to. They attempted to discourage us from adopting, saying we were not suitable parents. Eventually the government agreed. Taylor claimed himself as a single adoptive parent, leaving me to be considered nothing but a roommate or friend then he could adopt the children, and they would approve the documents. In our minds, we knew we were both their parents so we agreed. The whole process took many more months than it should have but eventually we were blessed with our two beautiful girls. At that point we were broke from the extra unnecessary expenses we were put through but at least we were together as a family. The wait and extra effort made it that much more rewarding when we finally reached our front doorsteps with them both in our arms.

Still flying by all the other cars, I told her to take the next exit and directed her towards the school. I was extremely grateful for her efforts, reminding myself to thank her greatly later when we had less on our hands. Knowing the time and realizing we might have missed them I knew I would have no one to blame but myself. Slowing slightly to go around the corner she ignored the mandatory flashing stop sign as we approached the school. I located the flag pole in the front of the school, high above the trees in the air knowing that that was where they were waiting. She slammed on her brakes. Stuck behind a ridiculously long line of other parents fighting with the busses to pick up their kids, I jumped out of the car and ran frantically down the road toward the school grounds, hoping that the kids were still sitting on the front steps of the school, waiting for me as usual.

I ran faster in between the cars that were lined up waiting for their turn to pick up their child. As I rounded the last car and came closer to the flag pole, I looked towards the stairs, glancing from child to child trying to pick mine out from the crowd. But I could not find my children. My eyes continued back and forth thinking I may have just missed them. Suddenly I heard a cry for help coming from behind me, a voice that was all too familiar to me. I whipped my neck around to catch a glimpse of a van door shutting. I immediately recognized that van as belonging to the Clements our next door neighbors. I ran quickly around a few more cars. Reaching the van I grabbed the handle firmly and yanked, trying to pull open the sliding door open.

No luck. The door was locked. I peered through the tinted window and saw my girls staring back at me a helpless look on their face. Yelling at them through the window to cover their faces, I began banging on the window. Over and over I threw my fists until finally smashing my fist through it. The glass shattered mostly the film from the tinting of the windows keeping most of the broken glass intact as I pushed it away. The adrenalin moved through my veins at the sight of my trapped kids, and the thought of what could have happened if I would have been even one minute later. Walking alongside the van with my body half way inside the window, I reached over to Ericka's waist trying to undo her seatbelt. Our neighbor, Mrs. Clements, began pushing my hands away and giving me a few punches in the face trying to discourage me. Hearing the clicking sound of the seatbelt, I grabbed Ericka, yanking her hard.

Mrs. Clements had her hands wrapped tightly around Ericka's legs. She thought that she was doing a favor to the children by getting them out of the home of two gay men, but she didn't know us. She was only judging off of predetermined generalizations and typical gay stereotypes that were completely false. She did not understand or even try to comprehend us and our family at all. She just assumed that the children must be in danger but were too afraid to cry for help. I yelled at her to let go of my child. At this point anyone who was not already watching from the school grounds was now staring right at us, not knowing what to do. I'm sure they were shocked at the sight of what all had just happened, and probably confused not understanding the story or the huge issue at hand. Parents were yelling at me having no clue what was going on. Letting go of Ericka with one hand, I swung my arm back smashing my fist into Mrs. Clements face, forcing her to release grip on Ericka's legs and grab her face in pain. The moment she let go Ericka jumped into my arms.

I began running with Ericka in my arms alongside the van, when one of the other children's teachers, who knew our situation, came up and took Ericka for me, promising she would protect her until I could return. Kissing Ericka on the forehead, I told her it would be ok before passing her off to Mrs. Freeman. Tears began flowing from Ericka's eyes, as I heard Naucia screaming out of fear, louder than I have ever heard a child cry. My thoughts returned to Naucia who was still stuck in the van, fighting with the old woman sitting in the front seat.

Naucia had undone her seatbelt hoping that I could pull her to safety the same way I had Ericka. Mrs. Clements was holding her on the other side of the van, too far in for me to reach. I stretched my hands out as far as I could, to touch Naucia's hands, when I caught a glimpse of the blood running down my arms from the few pieces of glass still protruding from my skin along my arms and torso. I was unable to even think about the pain, I knew I did not have much time left because the only car left in front of us was beginning to pull away. I tried jumping on the windows edge in order to reach inside the vehicle when the remaining glass in the window stabbed into my side. I scream out in pain and fell away from the car.

Mr. Clements sped up as we rounded the corner exiting the school yard, as I fell down into the curb. I slid across the pavement, looking up only to see the rear of the van pulling away. Another parent ran over to help me up, cuts and abrasions from the pavement all over my body. I limped toward the entrance where I had gotten out of the car. Walking across the grass island, the nurse spotted me limping toward her and pointing toward the van almost out of sight by this point. Her car squealed as she pulled up over the curb onto the grass, driving across the large island toward me tearing up the flower beds on her way. The door was wide open, swinging back and forth, as the car bounced toward me. I swung my body around the door pulling myself in and slamming the door closed. We drove across the grass and jumped the curb in pursuit of the van.

As the front end slammed over the curb sparks from the front fender scratching against the pavement shot over the hood and fizzled off into the air. As the back wheels fell off the curb, the back bumper was jerked off; I looked in the rear view mirror just in time to see the bumper spinning in the street. Turning back to look at her face, I wondered why she was going to all this effort for me. I sat there staring at her in awe of this woman, thinking she had to be mad, curious at the motivation behind her efforts. Our eyes met and she broke a smile of encouragement letting me know she was in this for the long haul. The engine revved as she pushed the pedal to the floor, making the loudest noise from an engine that I have ever heard. We flew past the stop sign not caring about any of the traffic laws. The tires screeched as we pulled out of the turn, the van now in sight, far away but still visible.

"Did I ever ask you your name?" I asked. Not knowing if I had. "I don't think so, now that you mention it," she replied. "My name is Latisha Brown," she said proudly with a smile on her face. "I'm," I spurted out before she interrupted me, "Bryan. I know who you are," reminding me of the turmoil with Taylor back at the hospital and the fact that I was her patient. "I think everyone at the hospital knows your name at this point," she said chuckling. "Well you and Taylor," she finished looking back at the road and focusing on the pursuit at hand knowing we still had a job to do. Dodging in and out of lanes we persisted in trying to catch up to the van, our minds focused on Naucia. We became stuck behind two cars blocking the road with no room on either side to squeeze our vehicle past. Latisha honked profusely at the vehicles demanding that they move. Eventually, the car on the left slowly crept up far enough in front of the other car to let us pass, flipping us off as we did. Latisha quickly returned the favor, giving me a slight chuckle.

I felt a sense of hope when I realized that there was only a handful more cars between us and the van. Returning the sole of her shoe to the worn out floor mat, slowly the car sped up. The speedometer obviously was broken reading 0 MPH. We cut off the last car, putting us right behind the van, almost close enough to be able to read the license plate number, although it was not needed as we already knew whose van it was and who was inside driving. Slowly inching closer, the car gave all it had. The engine roared as Latisha looked in my direction staring me in the eyes, and saying, "You're going to have to trust me, ok?" Before waiting for a reply she pulled the car to the right side of the van slamming the car's front bumper into the rear fender of the van. Turning the wheel to the side, the van slowly jerked until she slammed them once again sending them off into a spin, down into the ditch beside the road. My jaw dropped. Nothing at all came out my mouth as I screamed, silence, nothing, blank. It was as if their car was spinning out in slow motion wanting to flip over but God was firmly holding it right side up and letting it spin safely into the bottom of the ditch. She flipped the car around to park aside them, jumping out and running towards the van facing backward in a puddle of muddy slush..

    With one of us on each side of the van, we grabbed the sliding door handles and yanked on them. They were still locked. I reached my hand into the broken window, unlocked the door, swinging it open and reached for Naucia. Latisha, doing her nursing duty, grabbed her cell phone from her pocket and called 911, after seeing that Naucia was okay and in my care. She informed the dispatcher of the crash and the location, as I pulled Naucia into my arms holding her tightly to calm her fears. Wiping her tears away with my shirt as well as tears of joy from my face, I pulled her into my chest, holding her close, never wanting her to leave my arms again.

Chapter 6

Knowing the man was still there but not hearing a sound, Taylor turned his back to the wall and waited in silence. After a few moments had passed, the man cleared his throat desperately trying to detatch whatever flem was lodged inside. Taylor pressed his cheek firmly against the cement floor and stared through the crack. The man finally bent over, laid down on his stomach and brought his eyes up to the crack and spoke. After talking back and forth for some while the man knew that Taylor was not going to do well in here. He knew that if Taylor was to stay here he would only be another suicide on the other side of that wall and he was not about to let that happen again. "I've seen a lot of people come through here," he began telling me again, starting over from where he had left off from before and probably not remembering that he had already said it. "I've seen murderers, rapists, thieves, embezzlers, drug dealers. You name it, I've seen it, probably more than you could even imagine. I've seen it all," he continued. "I've seen all types of bad that exists in the world and let me tell you something," he said. His voice trembled a little obviously holding back his emotions, not wanting me to see that my story troubled him. A few moments passed before he began again, obviously forcing the words out. "You are not one of them," he said.

"You have not killed anyone. You did not steal. You did not even bring bodily harm to anyone." He said and Taylor knew he was right. All Taylor did was fight for the right to love and for the ones he loved. He was living his life as a civilized human being, following all the rules and laws of the land. Knowing the difference between right and wrong and living it as far as he was concerned. "I don't know the feelings of true love and I envy you for that." The man began again. "Even though I could say that I once tried to love a woman, I believe that your feelings are just as genuine as mine had been." It was as if he had to force out his words. I sat there trying desperately to catch what he was saying, as it was very hard to comprehend.

Pausing a few more moments, letting himself gain his composure, before he continued speaking again, "I have read a lot of newspapers that the guard would slip through the latch in the door a few times a week with my dinner. As I read the articles on the protest and fights for equality happening right outside these walls and all over the world, I am amazed of how passionate and determined you all are. I never took the articles to heart mostly because they did not pertain to me. I never understood what you all were fighting for or what the big deal was all about. To me never having a chance at it, marriage was just a word and definitely not something worth fighting for. But I get it. If I were you and that happened to me I'd be pissed too, that's fucked up." He said obviously having no one to talk to in here and more than happy to rant on and on. Taylor knew if he had equal rights and the opportunity for marriage, if he so chose, then he would have had hospital visitation rights and would not be here. "So, I want to help you and your kind in your fight." Bryan knew that however he helped him would also help every "second class" citizen or so they call us. "I have something to give you," he said after a few moments of debating it amongst himself.

Taylor was terribly confused wondering what he could possibly have being stuck in jail the last, who knows how many years. His jumper rustled as he reached into the pocket pulling out the item he wanted to give to Taylor. "Now you have to promise me one thing," he said with a pause waiting for him to respond. Slightly wanting to not accept the offer not knowing exactly what he was promising to Taylor answered "Yeah, ok," I said. "Everyone that comes in here has had plenty of chances to live right but they choose differently just like I did. But you're different. You live a good life even though everything's been against you. I'm giving you this because you don't belong here. You do not deserve to be here. I want you to use this to find your boyfriend, lover, husband." He said confused. Then do whatever you can to help people understand your people and treat them fairly. I want you to tell others the stupid shit you've told me. Go out and show the people how fucked up this is and what situations it is putting you guys in. If you tell them the story you just told me it might make a difference, I've never done much good in my life. I've never been much of a positive example to anyone, but maybe if I can help you inform others it would make up for the lousy person I have been. Someday I want to see a newspaper slip through the door with your picture on it telling the facts then I'll feel like I helped in making a difference for good in the world. Can you do that for me?"

Then he slipped a badge through the crack of the wall. Taylor grabbed it as fast as he could and held it against his heart. He thought of Bryan and their kids flooded in, not pausing to think of any consequences, just all the benefits. Taylor was still not sure if Bryan was even alive but he knew that he could not waste any time. Taylor's eyes filled with tears, as he thanked the man over and over again. Trying to keep himself calm he focused on how he was going to get out. The cell next to Taylor was quiet, as the old man sat there allowing himself to feel proud of what he had just done. Still holding the badge close to his heart, Taylor said, "Thank you," to the man again. "Thank you so much. I appreciate this more than anything in this world. There is nothing I would want more than to see my family again. This means so much to me. Thank you," Taylor said as he then thought to himself yes, I will keep that promise. I will go out, tell my story, and help people understand the necessity for equality and I won't stop until they listen. I promise one day you will see me on the front page Taylor thought not once thinking that this man may be bluffing the whole idea.

His clothes shuffled. "Now listen." The man said in a low scheming whisper. "I know you're excited and want to just bust out of this place as soon as you can, but it is not going to work that way. If you do it now you will get caught. There are no inmates in our corridor and they will spot you on the cameras instantly. After that they will bring you back here, but for a much longer period of time then you have now. So if we're going to do this, you're going to have to do exactly what I say and at the right time or you will screw it up and get caught." "Okay," Taylor agreed before the man had a chance to finish. He knew the man had been here much longer than he had and he knew much more of the ins and outs of this unreasonable place. Pushing himself closer to the wall, he listened intently to the plan. Taylor went over it a few times with the man repeating it back and forth to make sure they both had the exact same plan to eliminate any sort of confusion or mistakes. Knowing they were both prepared and ready, Taylor thanked him again and sat in the corner. Taylor stared at the small amount of light left in the room, waiting until it was time, knowing they would only have one shot.

The sound of the door blared through the corridor. All of the inmates knew that it was their last break for the days last chance to stretch their legs before they all had to retire back to their cells for the remainder of the night. The sound of the door alarm echoed off the walls, and as it slowly faded Taylor could hear the footsteps of the guard just outside his door, keys jingling on his thigh as he walked to the other side of the corridor. The sound of his steps fading as he got farther and farther away from his cell. "You remember the plan?" The old man whispered from the other side of the wall. "Yeah, I do, and thank you again," Taylor said back hoping this would work and he could return with gratitude for this man. One of the guards yelled across the corridor to all of us, "Thirty minutes." It was his way of letting us all know how long of a break we had to do our business. Another siren went off this time from the back side of the corridor.

Taylor rehearsed what the old man had told him, both guards had to be pushing their sirens to make the doors open. If anything was suspicious, only one had to release his hand from the button and both the doors would close immediately. The florescent lights from the hall shown through Taylor's door as it slowly slid open quickly piercing the room with beams of hope. All the doors banged loudly throughout the halls as they opened seconds apart from each other. Taylor stood up focusing his thoughts on only the plan. This was his only chance he kept thinking to himself determined to pull it off without any mistakes. A few men in orange jumpsuits passed by Taylor's door flooding their way toward the break room as he gathered himself onto his feet. He leaned against the wall, having not used his feet for quite a while they were still very weak. Stepping one foot out of the door, he joined the rest of the men gathering in the hall, slowly walking toward the break room.

Focusing most his energy on just trying to stay on his feet, Taylor wondered how in the hell he was going to pull off this plan. He kept one foot in front of the other as if it was his first time walking. Giving a generous amount of room on his left side for the others to pass him, he quickly glanced behind him in hopes that he could catch a glimpse of the old man that had quickly become his hero. His eyes shot from inmate to inmate trying to pick out which one he could possibly be, but no luck. He brought his eyes back in front of him to assist in his stability, falling over would only bring unneeded attention to him, which would ruin the plan. Keeping focused on the doorway and the inmates flooding through it, he went over the first part of the plan one more time in his mind before he had to execute it. One faulty move and he would be caught, and it would all be over.

His feet started moving faster and more relaxed as he inched closer to the door. He gazed into the other cells, all of which looked exactly the same; empty, bare and dingy. He kept telling himself not to make eye contact with any of the inmates, afraid that they might hurt or assault him, since he did not have enough energy to defend himself in a brawl, making him an easy target. Progressing through the doorway, the guard stood next to the metal frame, making sure everything was going smoothly. He was ready to release his button just adjacent to the door at any moment and lock off the hallway if anything were to happen. This would lock the problem inside, keeping it contained. If other inmates in the break room knew that there was an issue to be dealt with in another room needing more guard's assistance, making less security where they were, it would cause a mass ruckus. Approaching a small hallway on his right after passing through the metal doorway, Taylor looked back. The guard was still standing on the other side of the door, keeping an eye on the inmates exiting the corridor.

All the inmates continued to walk down the hall as Taylor slipped around the corner. Outstretching his hand with the badge firmly gripped, he beeped the badge across the access panel, granting him entrance into the small room. Closing the door slowly behind him, Taylor prayed that no one had seen him. He was putting all his trust in the old man, him and his plan. Taylor did not notice a camera in the hallway, which definitely did not mean that there wasn't one, just that he could not see it. He was going to have to trust the man when he said they would not notice him, remembering back inside his cell, when the man was explaining that the cameras do not reach that close to the hallway. They are placed to see you walk down the other ends of the hallway like he had done, but with a massive amount of people, they would not be able to notice one missing. As the door clicked shut, Taylor pressed his back firmly against the brick wall and listened to the others pass by. Their footsteps vibrated the tile floor in the hallway all the way to where he was standing. He could feel his heart pounding in fear. Trying to relieve his anxiety he took a moment to think back on our wedding day, one of the happiest days of our lives, stopping himself after a moment and acknowledging that he had a long way to go before he would be out of there and into my arms.

Glancing at the clock hanging on the back wall in the small room, he checked the time and then looked around one more time for the items that the old man had said he was going to need. The noise in the hallway stopped abruptly. The metal door made a loud unmistakable bang. The noise echoed through the corridor leaving the hallway and the small room in complete silence. Taylor's eyes jumped back to the clock, timing himself perfectly making sure he was giving the guards exactly three minutes to check the hallways for stragglers and walk back to the break room. Following the plan as precisely as he could he watched the minute hand, click and stop, click and stop, over and over. His eyes starting to play games on him as the minute hand looked as if it was clicking backward, or stalling on the same number. Frustrated that it would not go faster, he anxiously awaited afraid he would give himself away when he stepped outside the door. The minute hand slowly clicked past the three o'clock line indicated on the clock. "Ten more seconds," he said quietly to himself. Keeping his eyes on the clock he could hear the clicks in his mind as it got closer and closer to the time to activate the plan. "Three, two, one," he whispered to himself. Taylor glanced through the rectangular window in the door to make sure there was no one out there that would see him walking around the small room. Convinced it was clear, he grabbed a shirt hanging on the metal rack attached to the wall, unbuttoned his orange jumpsuit and pulled off his shoes.

The floor was cold, only slightly warmer than the concrete in his cell, sending shivers up his body at the thought of how long some people were actually here. Taylor quickly threw the shirt over his back forcing his arms through the slightly tangled sleeves. He grabbed some slacks folded and placed neatly on the shelf, for the first time not caring how they fit his body or that they hung a lot lower on his hips than he would have preferred. Gripping the back of his shoes he pulled them on then looked back at the clock staying keenly aware of the strict time schedule he was on. Noticing that he had about four minutes to spare, he fixed the cuffs of the shirt and pulled the end of his slacks over his shoes to hide as much of them as possible. He was not exactly sure what types of shoes were standard for this job, but he knew it wouldn't be the shoes of an inmate like he had on. Locating a mirror on the far wall, he took advantage of it and fixed his hair slightly. Obviously there was not enough time to make it look amazing, like he did every morning in front of the mirror for almost an hour but it would do. As he was snapping up the last button, he noticed a name badge on the left side of the shirt where a pocket should have been. "Carlos" was written in big black letters embroidered across a white tag. "Thank you Carlos," he said with a slight accent, smirking a little as he did.

Picking his jumpsuit up off the floor, he rolled it up into a ball and placed it in a black garbage sack and tied off the end to make sure the nasty bright orange would not catch anyone's eyes as they passed and tossed it into the garbage by the door.

Grabbing the badge from the shelf, Taylor attached it onto his shirt, flipping it backward so that the actual guard's picture was not showing. Looking at the clock, waiting for the right time, nervous as hell, he grabbed the handle and pulled the door open. Taylor was scared to death, trying hard not to let it show as two men walked by him in the hall. They did not even look at his face, assuming he was just a janitor because of his clothes and less significant to them, they walked by with their pride on their belts along with their gun, handcuffs and badge. In reality this was normal for Taylor, normal to get shunned and have people look away or scorn him just because he was gay.

Without hesitation Taylor turned the corner and began walking down the hall, luckily going away from where they were going and away from where he had just come. Taylor had to restrain from the urge to walk at a more brisk pace or even wanting to run, knowing that it would only attract unneeded attention. Keeping his speed at a semi normal working pace, not too fast or too slow, he did not want to look lazy and like he was not actually working or awkwardly quick for a janitor pace. He tried to remember the directions that he had been given by the old man, repeating them over and over to himself as he walked down the hall. Taylor noticed but did not look at the cameras strategically placed in the halls capturing every movement he was making. He kept his eyes on where he was going looking as if he had done it thousands of times before placing his sights on the wall straight ahead of him remembering that he had to turn and go left down the hallway on the backside of the break room where no one would be able to see him.

As he turned the corner looking down yet another long white brick hallway, it made him think of how many different color schemes they could use to make this place more vibrant and alive. Chuckling he reminded himself that that was not the point of a jail facility. His mind wandered back to the time when Bryan and he remodeled their kitchen and backyard, with the help of the kids of course. Laughing to himself he thought back to how the kids were not much help and actually made it much more difficult but a lot more fun in the long run. He remembered the little things they had done in the remodeled rooms that they were so proud of. Every time someone new came to our home the children would make them go and admire that very thing that they had done to contribute even going as far as to claim their small contribution, usually a tile placed by them, a rock or even a plant in the back yard, as the focal point of the whole space. Bryan and I would toy with them and joke that it really was the focal point, just to make them proud. Bryan and I both knew that none of their contributions were the focal point by any means, but it was a fun way to build their self esteem and the feelings of a job well done, Taylor thought.

Bringing his thoughts to the present Taylor again noticed the brightly lit overly baring white hallway, the double doors just ahead. The old man had said to pay attention because the doors opened to an identical looking hallway to the one he was in. Taylor came closer to the doors with every passing step his footsteps echoing off the walls, before fizzling off into silence, being absorbed into the cold moist air. Straight ahead, a short distance down the hall, Taylor began searching for the access panel, where he was to beep his badge, granting him access and opening the automatic doors. Locating the panel he bent over with his badge, which was clipped on his chest pocket, and passed it in front of the panel until he heard it beep. He immediately stepped back raising his arm to have the second sensor accept his existence in front of the door. Placing his hand in front of the red ring hovering it there for a moment, he waited patiently but nervously for the panel to activate and turn green.

His heart was racing as he stepped back thinking that the sensors above the doors may have detected that he was too close and disconnect the power from opening the doors as a safety feature. If he was too close, the doors would not open, preventing them from hitting him or any items that were in the way. Taking another step forward, he removed the badge from his breast pocket and swiped it by the access panel again before placing his hand back on the red ring praying to God that this time it would work. Sweat started to drip down his face like water in a red rock canyon after a short rain burst. His thoughts spiraled out of control as he assumed the worst. Had they realized his lack of presence in the break room? Did they notice him on the cameras? He was disappointed in himself and knew that he had let me and the kids down as tears began to fall from his eyes. Raising his hand slowly to wipe the tears from his eyes he noticed the ring on the panel now illuminated with a pure green ring, as the doors swung open. He wiped the remaining tears away from his face and realized he was one step closer to physical freedom. He looked around proud of what he had done so far and stepped through the door.

Chapter 7

Reattaching the badge to his right breast pocket, he glanced back at the doors as they automatically came to a brisk close behind him securing the hallway once again. Taylor was able to hear the chattering and visiting from the break room on the other side of the wall just as the old man had said he would. He stared down each of the next few halls he passed, hoping to catch a glimpse of the kind man that had renewed his hope in life, by giving him this chance. Taylor thought of the promise he had made to the man, promising to himself that he would keep it. He did not want to let him down, he had been holding onto that badge for God knows how long and it wasn't going to be in vain. "I will make the front page," Taylor said, in a grateful voice directed through the wall of the break room where the man was sitting. Taylor continued down the hall not knowing how or when he would be able to fulfill the promise, but knowing reassured somehow he would. The noise of his footsteps echoing off the walls made him more nervous with every step. He wished he was wearing something with a slightly less clicking sound as it was only distracting him, but he knew he had no choice in the matter and would live with that he had.

Staring down the hallway illuminated by only a few fluorescent lights and no windows, the hallway was slightly darker but felt more secure. Two men appeared from one of the adjacent hallways going in the same direction just ahead of Taylor, slowing his pace down slightly, and keeping him once again on a more normal walking pace instead of rushing as he had been before. He was afraid that he may be ahead of schedule and thanked God silently for sending them at the exact moment to slow him down and avoid the awkwardness and visibility of him standing at the end of the hallway, waiting for the signal to continue on with the plan. The two men stopped, pausing at the door. Taylor was not exactly sure what they were doing or what they may be thinking.

Looking at each other and laughing, they realized that they had both assumed that the other was going to beep the door open. The taller of the two men reached out slipping his card against the panel, opening the door. They both walked through leaving Taylor once again the only one in the hall. The thought of someone being able to see him on the camera would normally bother him considerably but in this unusual circumstance it was reassuring that they were the only ones, for now. After he passed through the front doors and left the building, the video of him walking down the hall would be watched by thousands. All of them wondering how he did it, how he outsmarted them. Having only been in here less than a day and still being able to escape right out from under their noses without even being familiar with the building; that was something he thought proud of himself. The video would be shown all over the news warning people and trying to get any clues to where Taylor could possibly be. A shallow smirk came across his face feeling proud of himself for doing this. He thought back to all the other feats he had accomplished in his life that most people could not even dream of. His life was definitely not the easiest, but without it being difficult and hurtful he would have accomplished very little. He was proud of most of his actions in his life, especially when he stopped lying to himself and others about his sexuality and finally came out. He lost his family, but he gained self respect, happiness and the desire to live again when he was true to himself.

He was sick of going through the motions of life, wanting to end it on a daily basis, just because he had different feelings than the rest of his family and friends. He was shunned, disregarded and tossed aside, all because he was attracted to someone that to them was unacceptable. He hated his life and wanted it to end. Taylor remembered planning how he would do it many times, each time coming closer to succeeding. Until he loved himself and accepted himself for who he was, he would never be happy. So he let go of others feelings toward him. He knew it was only going to get worse when he said he was gay. Most things get worse before they get better and he knew that. Taylor remembered one time specifically after coming home from a church function where the kids had ganged up on him. Teasing him and calling him a faggot. That comment cut him deeply, and he ran home crying. Entering the kitchen, he wiped his tears away, trying to make it look like nothing was wrong just in case anyone was home, not wanting them to ask any questions.

Running up the old wood stairs, two at a time, towards his parent's room he planned to end his life. He could not comprehend why the people at the church, where they preached tolerance and love on a weekly basis, were the ones that were the most intolerant. He was sick of feeling like he was a horrible person, being cast down for having feelings, which he was born with and never chose in the first place. He went through this torture day after day at school and at church, being ridiculed and mocked for being different.

Sliding his father's bottom drawer open, Taylor rummaged through it, pushing his underwear aside, revealing the black handgun. He knew it was in there and had planned on using it many times before. His father had placed the gun there to protect his family in case an intruder broke in and tried to harm them, but today, instead of protecting them, it was going to be the reason for the harm. Taylor gripped the gun firmly and felt the cold metal against the inside of his hand sending chills throughout his body. Soon it would be all over. All the mocking, the teasing, the abuse, the torment, it would all be over, and he would return to the place he originated from, to live in a judgeless world, free of discrimination and hate.

Grabbing the bullets from another drawer in the chest, he placed them both in the pocket of his hoodie and ran back down the stairs, forgetting to close the drawers, not caring that he forgot. By the time his parents noticed that they were open and that the gun and bullets were gone, he would already be dead. Reaching for the keys hanging on the hook in the kitchen, he swung the back door open frantically jumped into the family car and drove up the street to the mouth of the canyon. He drove up the canyon road that he had driven up so many times before but never for this particular reason. Usually he would just drive up to think and ponder about his life and his feelings. This time he debated over life itself, knowing this would be the last time he would ever have to do so. A short distance up the road, he veered off the main canyon onto a small dirt road that led to a somewhat remote location, out of sight from the nearby homes, overlooking the valley below covered with beautifully colored trees and ponds.

Stopping the car and stumbling out, tears rushed down Taylor's face as he yelled at the world. Mad at God for not understanding why he would put him in this position wondering why his attempts to change were always unsuccessful, and why his prayers went unanswered. "If God wanted me to be straight, like the bible says man is supposed to be, then why won't God help me change? Did he not care? Was God even there?" Taylor cried as he knelt down, placing his hands on a rock in front of him, praying once again harder and more sincere than he ever had before. Without an answer now, it would be his last prayer.

Taylor spoke to God as if he was standing in front of him, standing there staring, ignoring his plea for help. Taylor began yelling at him in frustration. Trying to get him to understand and help him this one last time before he gave up. Taylor felt as if God was standing directly on the other side of the rock he had his hands placed upon. His back turned toward him refusing to hear his prayer. Taylor wanted so badly to feel the same spirit that his parents and everyone in the church claimed they had felt, confirming to them that the church was true. He longed for the feeling of knowing without a shadow of a doubt that God was there, hearing every one of his prayers and answering them with love and compassion. He wanted that desperately.

But no answer came. Again only silence. Taylor reached into his pocket pulling out the handgun and bullets. He placed them on the rock in front of him as if to offer them to God, for him to take them away so he did not have to do this. Pleading with God to give him a sign, a feeling, something of significance, to let him know it would all be okay. The gun sat there as a few more minutes passed and Taylor realized the hopelessness of it all. He was gay, and God and everyone were ashamed of him for it. They did not understand that I did not choose to feel this way, they did not care to understand.

Picking up the gun and placing one of the bullets in the chamber, Taylor unlocked the safety with the bullet nestled securely inside. Looking toward the sky, the clouds rolled emotionlessly across. He said his final prayer knowing within moments when he pulled the trigger, his life as he knew it would be over. The turmoil, the struggle, the pain of just living, it would all be over. Finishing his final words he pressed the gun into his stomach, the part of his body he hated the most. Not wanting to die instantly but wanting God, if there was a God, to have to watch him slowly suffer as he laid there bleeding to death on the side of that small dirt road. He thought of the wonderful childhood he had there and about his mother and the good times they had had. "Goodbye," he mumbled out tasting the salt from his tears as he pulled the trigger. The bullet roared out of the gun, tearing through his shirt, ripping his skin open and thrusting itself into Taylor's body. Shattering every dream he had ever had in life as it blasted through his organs before exiting through the back of his body. Taylor's goals and aspirations now gone along with the agony and the pain of living day to day. He pulled his hands away from his stomach and the entry point of the bullet, his hands covered in blood, his body fully numb fell to the ground, his sight became blurry, and with no regrets for what he had done he lost consciousness.

Taylor shook his head trying to get that dreadful memory out his mind. He hated his past, as did Bryan and almost every other gay man they had ever come in contact with throughout both their lives. He shook his head again, more vicious this time, trying desperately to rid his mind of the past, of the suicide attempt, and of the wretchedly hatful days after in the hospital with his family, and focus on the here and now. He needed to get out of there and find Bryan, those thoughts were the only ones he wanted in his mind. Scanning the walls to locate a clock trying to keep himself on schedule, he rounded the last corner of the hallway. Not knowing how he was doing on time, thinking he might be a little behind because of the hold up from the uncooperative door. He was sure the old man did not plan on him being an idiot, for letting that happen. Even if he hadn't, he would have no clue how to incorporate them into the plan. He could only plan based off of how long it had taken him to walk the path when he walked it with the guards.

He had no way to know what to expect of Taylor, and Taylor had no way to know what to expect at all. He was glad he had gotten through what he had so far and was still progressing unnoticed in Carlos' janitorial outfit. Taylor focused on the stopping point the man had designated, further down the hall. This was the point Taylor should be at when the old man would cause a ruckus in the break room requiring the guards to run in and stop the fight. Having all the guards and cameras focused on that situation alone would leave Taylor free to exit the last closely watched door unseen.

Keeping his adrenaline level in control, wanting desperately to run, Taylor forced himself to stay at a normal pace. He could see his next destination just ahead of him. He was almost there, he was so close. Every thought that came into his mind kept returning to Bryan and his condition. Was he ok? Was he even alive? Taylor thought. For all Taylor knew I could be fine, or I could have been dead hours ago. He continued walking down the lonely hallway, spotting the cameras in the corners knowing they could see him. Taylor forced himself to maintain his composure and not give into his instincts to look back at them. All he could hope for was that they saw a typical janitor who cleaned the jail on a daily basis and not an inmate trying to escape. The lights flickered for a moment before illuminating back to full fluorescent brightness, reflecting off the white brick walls and the shiny, speckled, off white floor. When all of a sudden a bright red light started flashing on the wall ahead of him, above the last door that was slowly closing. He was late, Taylor thought to himself, the door was closing because the old man started the fight in the break room. Taylor ran towards the door knowing that he had to make it through before it closed, locking him in and the rest of the world out.

Chapter 8

The light flashed every few second as the door was slowly closing. Not caring what the guards watching him from the cameras may think, Taylor began to run down the hall. If that door closed and he was not on the other side, his whole attempt would have been in vain. Getting through that closing door was his only chance for survival. Sprinting toward the opening, he realized it was going to be a tight squeeze by the time he reached it. As he approached to the door, Taylor turned his body sideways; it was the only he was going to make it through the small crack. Taylor released the air in his lungs compressing his chest as flat as possible, thinking if his chest made it through, the rest of his body should also. The door continued to slide from inside of the wall to the other, quickly closing off the hallway.

Even after releasing all the air, his chest still brushed along the side of the door, popping off a few buttons from Carlos' shirt. Taylor's body scratching along the side of the door pulled him down onto the floor. His head smashed onto the clean floor spewing spit from his mouth as if he had been punched by a boxer on the side of the face. His shoulders pounded against the floor, followed by his hips and the rest of his lower body. His body bounced more than once across the floor, before coming to a stop a few feet away, pressed up against the wall. Immediately he thought of the guards. Had they seen him? Had they seen what had just happened? Taylor took a large breath and mumbled out one last goodbye and one last thank you to the old man still fighting for him inside.

As the door was about to close, Taylor saw something shiny reflecting on the other side of the door. Pressing his face up against the wall he tried to get a glimpse of the shiny object before the door closed completely. Unable to recognize the item, the door came to a piercingly loud bang. Removing his battered face from the floor he leaned against the wall for support. His feet were shaking, head pounding from the trauma a few seconds before as he turned to walk away. The sound of the siren continued to blare through another long hallway ahead, empty except for Taylor and the flashing red light. Squinting his eyes Taylor tried to get a better look to see where the hall led, as there were no more turns or hallways in the originated plan.

Taylor saw what he believed to be more doors, but they looked nothing similar to any of the doors he had seen thus far. The doors were shiny as if made of glass. Could it be a possible way to the outside? He squinted to get a better look as he walked forward, one hand firmly placed against the wall helping stabilize himself. His feet were stumbling over themselves, after having the fall he had just had. This brought back memories of his earlier drunken days fighting gravity just to keep his body erect. The mere idea of those days reminded him of why he had not gotten that drunk again for the last twenty years. As he thought back to those days, the fond memory of the first time he met Bryan came to mind as well.

Taylor recalled the excitement he felt as one of his best friends told him all about Bryan and what he was like before their blind date. Just before Bryan arrived at his friend's house where Taylor was already waiting, his so called friend informed him he had to go see his potential new boyfriend. He apologized profusely about having to leave Taylor at his house to meet Bryan without him, but reassured him that his younger sister would be there to help cut the tension of their first meeting.

When Bryan came over they sat on the curb trying to decide what to do. Since their mutual friend had ditched them and was the one with the plans for the night, they decided to drive around town. Being late in the evening, the shops and stores had already closed for the night, so they headed up into the mountains for a peaceful summer drive. The conversation was rough as they tried to think of things they had in common besides the so called mutual friend that had left them earlier that night. As they reached the top of the canyon, the conversation picked up slightly. It was pitch black when they parked the car and walked up a short trail before coming upon an unattended smoldering log in a round fire pit. The large log in the center was still glowing as they placed a few smaller pieces of wood on to start the fire back up once again. After the fire had begun to illuminate the forest around them, their conversation bloomed into an ever growing fire as well. Talking to each other as if they had known one another for years and at that exact moment Taylor knew without a doubt that Bryan was the one he was going to be with the rest of his life.

Taylor knew Bryan needed him more than ever right now and that nothing could stop him from reaching him. As all of the amazing memories of their past flowing through his mind, the thoughts of the fight they had had that morning kept repeating vividly in Taylor's mind. He desperately wanted to apologize for what he had done, to let him know that he was sorry and still loved him. Taylor refused to let his last words to Bryan be out of anger. The hall was still empty too full of Taylor's thoughts and emotions for him to even notice. The noise from the break room had now fizzled away locked behind by the large steel door that he had recently been assaulted by. The grand lobby slowly opened up into a brilliant granite coliseum which was a stark contrast to the dark cells behind me. Taylor was still slightly limping from the run in with the steel door, but rays of relief went

82

throughout his whole body when he saw the outside world only a few a steps away. "Antonio," a voice shouted out from across the lobby. "Antonio," the voice bellowed again. Taylor looked over his right shoulder back toward the man clearly yelling at him.

The short unshaven man continued toward Taylor as he began to walk slightly more briskly toward the doors leading to his freedom. He was not going to be questioned after coming this far. "Antonio," Taylor heard once more as the man grabbed his shoulder and turned him vigorously around panting under his breath. "God your deaf," he said. Taylor kept his head faced down towards the ground hiding himself. "I heard you're new here," he said putting his hand out to greet Taylor as he introduced himself. "I'm Mark, one of the security guards here." Reaching his hand out and shaking for an awkwardly long period of time before the man began asking more questions trying to be a overly friendly coworker. "How was your first day? Did they make you do grunt work like they made me do? They made me do stupid little jobs for like the first week till they hired the next guy and then he took over doing it all and I finally got to do what I was actually hired to do," he said in one breath trying to get in as much as possible before taking another breath and continuing on with his annoying questions.

Taylor was glad he didn't have to answer, knowing that it might give him away. "Did you see the fight in the break room?" He asked obviously very excited about it. Taylor realized the man was not going to shut up anytime soon and knowing that he had more important things to do and could not stand here all day listening to him mutter on with his nonsense, he touched the man's shoulder giving it a slight pat, turned around and began walking away without saying a single word. Taylor prayed that he would not try and follow him not only because he would give Taylor away but also because he was so annoying. "Well, see ya tomorrow," the man yelled out much louder than necessary allowing the whole crowd of people in the rotunda to hear him. Taylor looked back over his shoulder trying to cover himself up wondering who the hell this kid was. He pushed the door open and passed the guards on his left, who were busy scanning people for guns and weapons, sliding bags and briefcase through the scanners and slowly walking people through the metal detectors.

The next step Taylor placed was the sole of his shoe on the cement walkway below engraved with the names of soldiers and people who had served our country to give us the freedom we have as Americans citizens today. Many of which Taylor was not entitled to as a gay man and he knew it. Taylor took in a breath of fresh air as if it was the first time doing so in twenty years and for many of the inmates it very well may have been. He kept his movements at a steady pace while making his way to the edge of the long newly painted asphalt parking lot. He envisioned the route he was going to take to the hospital, assuming Bryan was still there and hopefully in good condition. Taylor tried to plan his next few moves in his head, because the man in the cells plan stopped as soon as he pushed open the glass door leading to the exit. Putting the parts of the plan together from where he was, to how he was going to get past the nurse's station, which had started this whole issue. Taylor knew the hospital staff would recognize him a lot better than the jail personnel did, since they had already seen him a few hours before. To the normal person this plan altogether would have been utterly hopeless, and unnecessary, but to Taylor, a gay man, having already been through a lot and fighting everyday just to be alive, it seemed to all come together with ease. He knew the hospital would be the hardest hurdle that lay ahead, but he was ready for the challenge.

He was sure that the entire hospital staff had heard of what had happened and would be watching Bryan's room with much more fascination than any of the others. Once out of sight from the jail, Taylor began to run. He ran faster than he had ever run before, reminding him of the story that Bryan's grandmother had told us of when she ran to the man she loved. Taylor thought to himself that he was really part of her family, carrying on her tradition of fighting for truth and running for love. His feet felt as if they were not even touching the ground, as if he was being carried by an angel of God, Bryan's grandmother's spirit, or even the essence of someone who had been through this exact same situation before. Someone that had been in his shoes, and felt the discrimination and persecution that Bryan and he felt, someone who had also been gay, and who is now just trying to help out "family". Taylor had a feeling that his time was running out faster that he could run, or be carried. The guards at the jail would soon, if not already, figure out that his cell was empty and he was gone. They would immediately come searching for him, first in the jail itself, checking all the videos in the break room and other areas where the inmates in his hall were located, and eventually they would find video of him and his route to the exit. He now realized that he hadn't thought this through thoroughly, but he knew now that it was too late to look back and change it, he was doing this. The anxiety produced from that thought pushed Taylor that much more. His heart beat faster from the adrenalin, as well as the exertion his body had gone through and was still going through in order to reach the man he loved.

Taylor had not been down in this area of town that often and was going to have to base this part of the plan off of pure inspiration. He elected to take roads that were the most concealed, covered by trees and taller buildings. Maneuvering his way through the town Taylor went back and forth between streets, trying to keep himself in anything but a straight line, hoping that his presence would be unnoticed. Taylor continued this pattern until he recognized a familiar road, a popular restaurant or something else he knew to base his direction and next move off of. About a mile or so away from the jail now, his progress slowed. With the reduction in pace, he began taking smaller untraceable roads. Many of them did not even have street signs or addresses on the buildings. Alleys and back roads of buildings became his best plan and he began executing it taking any no name streets. He continued running meandering his way through the unfamiliar part of town before reaching the river that divided the town into equal halves and he knew the hospital was on the other side.

Taylor found one of the many bridges strewn all along the river to let drivers access the other parts of town. Grabbing the side railing along one side of the bridge that was made specifically for pedestrians he flung himself around and began to run once again across the bridge toward the other side. Reaching the crest of the bridge that over looked the normally rapidly moving dirty green water, he looked down, and today the water had chunks of ice and slush covering its top. Taylor gazed forward once again. His body stopped in its own tracks as if he had just landed in a pool of hardening cement. He stood there staring at the police vehicles and personnel waiting on the other side of the bridge. He backed up beginning to turn around hoping they had not seen him. "Get on the ground," a demanding voice called out from one of the officers.

Taylor's heart began to pound faster and harder as it dropped to his stomach trying to drown itself inside. Turning to run he saw a group of five or six police officers closing in from the side that he had just come from. Along with the police vehicles was an old beat up car, Taylor was unsure what it was doing there with the police vehicles. He stood still in the middle of the bridge looking over at the river once again. He could not be caught without making the front page and without seeing Bryan once again but He was surrounded by police officers on both sides of the bridge, officers that were unable to see each other due to the arc of the road. Taylor thought about doing what many gay men have done before him and jump with the intention of ending their lives. He realized that he if he did not jump, then one of the two sides of police groups would catch him. He walked closer to the edge preparing to jump. He knew that the impact would surely end his life, but he remained optimistic of making the front page which would let Bryan know he did not give up on him, and that he pushed till the end.

"If I were to survive," Taylor quickly thought to himself, "I'm sure I would be injured severely, not only from the fall but also from hypothermia due to the freezing temperature of the water. It is sad to think but that was my ultimate goal, the officers would have to take me to the hospital to reconstruct my broken body before taking me back to jail. Maybe while I was there I would see Bryan one last time." Taylor placed one foot on the cement barricade ready to jump, while people shouted from all around him knowing what he planned on doing. Some of them trying to do their job and stop him others calling for back up to get ready for a water rescue. Taylor began to say his last goodbyes' pleading with God to let him survive. This act reminded him of the last time he had pleaded with God as a child before shooting himself, although this time he was in a much different mindset, and he knew that he was not going to be found by a group of motorists and saved like last time. This was different. His arms began gripping the pole as he was ready to jump up and over the barricade in front of him as someone yelled out. The voice stood out from all the rest, stopping him in his tracks, "Taylor," they yelled.

Chapter 9

My blood was fully darkened on Latisha's husband's shirt and pants, as well as dried to my skin and the hair on my arms and legs. I was not looking forward to scrubbing it off afraid it would painfully rip, pulling and peeling my skin off. I sat down in the passenger seat of Latisha's car; Naucia was still on top of me squeezing her arms around my neck as I held her tight. I closed the passenger door ready to continue this wretched day unaware of what may be ahead. Latisha was checking on the Clements making sure they were okay. Checking the vitals and consciousness of both of them, she helped them situate themselves back into their seats to keep their bodies from further injuries. Turning the van off before running back toward us and jumping in the car, she plopped herself in the driver's seat, bouncing the old broken car a little as she entered the car. "I'm a church going woman," she said. "I couldn't just let them sit there and die." I nodded in agreement knowing that she was right. I was furious at the Clement. I wouldn't have been able to do the same after what they had done to my family all of these years. She kept revving the engine more than normal for that car and much more than normal for any other car, just to get the care started. We pulled out of the ditch and up onto the road and drove back toward the school.

Naucia never looked up, her head pressed against my chest, my arms tightly around her back in a tight loving hug. I began to comfort her and let her know that everything would be okay now that she was back in my arms. I never wanted to let go of her again, thinking that only a few different moves on our part and she could have been gone forever. "Naucia," I said as we pulled around the last corner, the school insight, "Help me find your sister," I asked her, the loss of blood finally catching up to me as I began to feel faint. My eyes felt heavy, but I refused to give into my body's wants. I kept my mind on the goal, focusing every ounce of energy I had left in me on Ericka and Taylor. As we passed the school's monument in the center of the grass island, the glare from the bronze statue of Thomas Lane, the founder of the school, and the letters below his feet reading Thomas Lane Academy illuminated back at me. Tire marks and turned up flowers became predominantly visible along the center island. Latisha turned the wheel echoing the squeaking of the axils throughout the car, as we began to round the half circle around the statue. I opened my eyes noticing the principal standing around the tire tracks in the grass staring at us with a stern look on his face. He did not know all that had happened, but I assumed he had heard that it was us from the look on his face, probably from the other bystanders.

About a quarter of the way around the half circle the stairs came into view. I began to look for the teacher I had handed Ericka to as my eyes began to unfocus slightly. I could make out her teacher sitting on the red painted curb. Ericka sat tightly on her lap, waiting for me to come back like I had promised her I would. She became wildly ecstatic to see Naucia and me in the front seat of the car. Ericka ran freely toward us, her hands stretched out toward me as she ran. It made me smile seeing her body leaning and bouncing side to side knowing she was unable to run in a straight line and knowing she never really wanted to. I opened the creaky door giving her full access as she jumped up onto my lap almost pushing Naucia off. I held both girls in my arms tightly, my head placed in between theirs resting on their shoulders. Tears began streaming down my face. "You're ok, dad's here, I've gotcha," I said reassuring both of them after all that they had gone through in the past hour or so. "I love both of you so much, I would never leave you," I said wanting them both to always remember that, as the teacher arrived with Ericka's backpack.

"Oh my God," she said in a slow disgusted voice not knowing what else to say. "You guys okay?" She continued looking down at my blood covered clothes. "Yeah, we're fine," I replied releasing my grip on the girls slightly to enable myself to see her as she leaned over to see into the car herself, judging us for a moment for what we were driving. "What was that all about?" She asked before interrupting herself to ask me if I was okay once more, obviously seeing the massive amounts of blood closer this time. "You need to go to the hospital," she said as she reached into her pocket for her phone and proceeded to dial for an emergency ambulance. "No. I'm fine, really," I replied feeling a little fainter than before. Taylor was still the first thing on my list of priorities. "Bryan," Latish said, shifting her head and repositioning herself in the seat to look at me in the eyes, "She is right you have lost a lot of blood and you need to get medical attention back at the hospital." "No," I said in a stern voice, glaring at her in the eyes letting her know I was serious. "We need to find Taylor." Although she was driving she knew my mind was unchangeable. Before she could take me to the hospital she knew we would have to either find Taylor or she would have to wait for me to pass out from the loss of blood.

I held the girls in the front seat, their legs stretched out onto the dashboard in front of us. I could hear the blinker clicking as we rounded the corner onto the onramp not sure if the light of the blinker on the outside of the car worked or not. I could see the nurse gazing off, losing focus of the plan slightly. I could tell her thoughts were wondering by the look on her face as well as the speed we were going. Staring at her I wondered what she

90

could possibly be thinking. I caught her looking over at the girls on my lap a few times before she realized I could see her and jolting her head back to the road. This persisted for some time even after we had exited the highway. She finally looked at us all and asked the question that had obviously been on her mind for quite some time. "You two are so beautiful," she said looking at the girls trying to break the ice for the real question on her mind. "Thank you," the girls replied almost in unison not knowing what else to say. I did not even remember if I had introduced them. "How old are you two?" Latisha asked in an unusual tone of voice as if she was a detective and the girls were the culprits, interrogating them for answers. It sounded as if she already had a great knowledge of what she believed the answer was but tried to get proof from them that she was right.

The girls got shy as Naucia began to answer for both of them. "I'm seven and she is five." "Oh my god!" I yell out sitting straight up, interrupting the nurse's next question. She was obviously not paying attention to the road. Looking straight ahead I could see a cluster of police cars at the bottom of the bridge and immediately my heart sank. Somehow I knew exactly what they were doing. I could barely make out the person standing on top of the bridge but I knew without a doubt it had to be Taylor. The police officer tried to redirect us to a side street as we got closer to him motioning to us with his light stick. The nurse stopped the car. The police officer started to yell at her to continue moving the way he was directing her to go and to keep traffic flowing. I jumped out placing the girls back into the front seat before closing the door. The police officer looked at me knowing it was his job to stop me. He started to yell and began running after me. My eyes focused only on what I believed to be Taylor on top of the bridge in front of me. The police cars aligned in front of me. They saw me coming as they leaned forward bracing themselves for the impact and held me back. The other officers still had their guns drawn and pointed at the man on the bridge. "Let me go," I kept yelling over and over. I knew that Taylor needed my help and I was determined to succeed. Shoving them from side to side and inching my way out of their grasps, I had a gut feeling that something was terribly wrong and I had to stop it.

My intuition took over. I fought back and forth with the police officers as more came to assist. They crowded around me to secure my safety which was absolutely the last thing I needed, or wanted them to be doing at that precise moment. My body built up a sweat from the fight. Grinding my teeth together in frustration I continued to yell at them to release their grip and let me go. I know they heard me say it but they had no idea why it would be beneficial or even safe, for me or them. They were here to do a job, to capture an escaped criminal, and to protect the citizens of this state and make the criminal pay the time for the crime which he had committed. I saw my efforts to escape their grasps as a useless waste of my already very low energy level. I couldn't over power them to get to Taylor and I knew that. Even with the built up adrenaline at this time, the adrenaline I had was just enough to keep me standing. I conjured up some unused energy lurking somewhere in my body waiting for this moment I suppose. With that last bit of energy I yelled out at the top of my lungs, louder and stronger than ever, never having a reason to do it before, "Taylor!" I yelled, all my energy into that one simple word. I had said it millions of times before but never so loud that I could almost see the sound waves travel through the air toward him. Taking a deep breath from having just exhaled any and all remaining breath in my lungs, I smiled as I saw him. I was still gasping for breath. He turned his head toward me and caught a glimpse of me from the corner of his eye.

Continuing to turn the rest of his body, his eyes focused on me. He refused to blink, not wanting to waste a single moment especially in the circumstances we were currently in. Our emotions ran high as if it was the first time we had seen each other in years. It seemed as if the world was silent for a moment. His smile beaming toward me as I'm sure mine was beaming toward him. Back and forth voices were yelling from one officer to another, something was beginning to happen, when a shot rang out firing through the air from the other side of the bridge. Taylor's mouth opened gasping for air as he yelled out in piercing pain.

The bullet slashed through his chest ripping blood and tissue from where the bullet exited. His shirt started ruffling and waving back toward his body after being yanked away from him by the bullet that had entered and exited his torso. The blood was plainly visible from where I was being held captive surrounded by officers. The shirt he was wearing that I did not recognize immediately became covered in a dark red stain growing quickly in size as only seconds passed. Taylor looked up at me for what could very well be the last time our eyes would ever meet. Despair and anger was present in all of his facial features. He knew that he had let me and our children down. My heart stood still, I couldn't think, everything seemed unreal. My emotions came to a void. I could not even comprehend all that had just happened. I continued to stare at Taylor as his body plummeted to the ground. Taylor's knees were the first part of his body to smash into the ground, followed by his chest and face skidding along the pavement briefly before resting in its final position.

In the car Latisha was also stunned by what had just happened, as were the two girls who witnessed the whole thing and were devastated and confused at who would want to shoot their daddy. No one on this side had permission to shoot, and they were unaware of the officers' already on the other side. Their grip on me loosened, and I ran toward Taylor. The officers' reached out toward me but I was already too far away. They did not realize that they had let me go. Chasing after me with weapons drawn, ready to protect me and themselves in case Taylor tried to do anything or had any weapons on his person. Ascending to the top of the bridge, ten feet or so away from Taylor's body, I could see the officers' of the other side. They looked as confused as the officers' did on the side I had just run away from.

The Sergeant was yelling out at them, trying to figure out who had fired their weapon. I bent over as I approached Taylor lying face down on the pavement. I rolled him over carefully but quickly trying not to inflict any further pain. His head rolled over to one side limp. His eyes seemed lifeless as well. His body continued to rollover, following his head, in one large limp mass till coming to a rest on his back, head toward the sky. My hands were dripping with blood, unsure if it was my newly gushing injuries from the run up the bridge or from Taylor rolling over. I knelt into a puddle of even more of Taylor's blood, trying to find the initial bullet entrance to put pressure on it and stop the bleeding. I gazed into his eyes, deeply wanting him to look back at me. I began to lose hope; his eyes were wide open staring off into the distance behind me. He was as lifeless as could possibly be. It was as if he had been dead for days. They were glazed over in a very un-lifelike way. I shook him, yelling at him to come to and talk to me, to say something, anything that would give me a little hope. I grabbed his hand knowing that if he could feel his hand in mine and knew I was there; he might come back and fight just a little harder.

The officers' that had been restraining me only moments

before arrived shortly after I did to Taylor's side, and bent over Taylor's body to check for any signs of life. The nurse was not far behind, after realizing what had happened. She was the most educated to handle this situation. She ordered them to get out of the way so she could perform her duties and job responsibilities as a nurse. I watched her closely checking for any signs of life. The cops were still restraining me. About lifeless, I just stood there emotionally and almost physically dead myself, being held up by their strength alone. Blood from Taylor continued to drip from my arms meeting up with blood from my own injuries before continuing down my legs and onto the pavement below. I stood there waiting, waiting for a sign of life from Taylor. Anticipating that the ambulance would arrive and take us back to that horrid place where this had all begun. I felt as if my face would soon become a river from the tears that should be careening down, but the tears did not come. My body was too parched to produce a single tear. My partner was dying and I physically could not even shed a tear.

My eyes remained on Taylor, unable to remove them for even a second to glance over at our kids still sitting with their faces pressed up against the window of the car. My body was emotionally exhausted and done for the day, possibly the rest of the week, or even my life. I couldn't even complete the act of thinking a second into the future. The sound of sirens echoed through the buildings alerting cars of its fast approach, increasing in volume as it got closer and closer to us and our horrible situation on the bridge.

The sound of the sirens rang in my ears bouncing around inside of me refusing to get out. There was nothing I could do, I kept thinking to myself. Taylor loved me. He loved me so much that he fought the old lady at the hospital. He got tased and sent to jail, and possibly died all for me. This was my fault and there was nothing I could do, I thought to myself over and over again. I felt so useless. All I could do was stand there and pray for the best. Not wasting any time the EMT's pushed the back doors of the ambulance open and ran up the slightly steep road toward us in the middle of the bridge. Latisha yelled out to them all of the details and numbers she had on Taylor's current condition. She followed up with her credentials to let them know that she was a trusted source and the information was correct. Latisha assisted the two other EMT's in getting the stretcher ready for Taylor's body, lifting his body all together; they placed him down onto the stretcher. The material on the stretcher immediately soaked up his blood staining it red. They secured him down with straps and wasted no time in getting the stretcher down the road, into the ambulance and securing it down for the ride to the hospital.

Latisha clutched me pulling me away from the officers' and supported me as we ran down after Taylor and the group of EMT's. Latisha shouted out to me the whole time letting me know what I was to do next. Arriving at the ambulance Taylor was already loaded in and being attended to by one of the younger looking EMT's. Latisha assisted me in getting into the back, closing the doors behind me and yelling to the driver that we were all loaded in and ready to go. I stared out the back window at her as the ambulance drove off. She knew I had nothing left in me. She knew what she had to do for me and my family at this crucial time in our lives and she was doing just that. As she stood in the middle of the road with the look of hope and love on her face holding our girls at her side, I said one last prayer as we drove toward the hospital.

She was the only person that really knew all that we had been through today. She knew even more about our lives than Taylor and I did about each other's today. She now knew our whole lives, all the struggles that we have been through together.

She didn't know all of the great things or the true joy we have experienced as a family, but she did see the hardships. She had only shared one day with our family and it had taken not only an emotional toll, but also a physical toll on her body. Her face said it all as she stood there watching us drive away. Our eyes met with an emotional understanding and respect for one another, but both of us in a very different way. The look on her face truly showed that she had a better understanding of how hard this world can truly be for a gay couple trying to raise a family. I looked at her in gratitude once again for her service to me and my family.

Chapter 10

I sat on the steps outside the emergency room of the hospital with my face planted in my hands. My mind acting as a digital picture frame flipping back on all the photos and memories of all the great times Taylor and I had together. I reminisced about the family trips we had gone on together especially the ones with the kids. The pictures of us at Disneyland on Naucia's birthday and the memories of how excited we were when Ericka took her first steps, all of them kept replaying over and over in my head. The memories of our honeymoon that my grandmother had made possible and other memorable and intimate memories we shared together, kept flowing through my mind. It was only disrupted by the thoughts of Taylor lying in the hospital bed without me, without his kids, and without anyone that loved him.

My mind was racing with thoughts of all the things I could have done better. What could I have said or done to help him know just how deeply I loved him. Just then, I was interrupted by Latisha and the kids pulling up in the rusty old station wagon. Slowly coming to a screeching stop in front of the ER, parking just behind the ambulance I arrived in. Latisha yelled while getting out of the vehicle, "Why the hell are you out here?" "Get in there," she piped back at me before I had a chance to collect myself and answer her. She opened the back door for the girls to get out. "Same reason they told Taylor when he came to see me. Because we are not legally married or recognized." "That's bullshit," she yelled out, unaware that we tried not to swear in front of our girls. "What can we do? I have to see Taylor," I told her as my girls ran into my lap swinging their arms around me in a giant hug.

Tears filled the girls' eyes as they looked into mine knowing that this was not good. There was something terribly wrong and they grasped the concept that Daddy might not make it. She took a moment to think of any possible way around this, since she knew the rules and regulations much better that I did. We stared at each other for a few seconds until I saw the look on her face. It immediately told me without her saying a word that there was absolutely nothing she could do. "I'm sorry," she said knowing it would not change anything. It was the only thing she could say at a time like this. "Will you do me one favor?" I asked looking up at her. She sat next to me and put her arms as far as she could around all of us holding us tight. "Anything," she whispered as we huddled on the front steps.

"Will you," I began. Crying so hard I could not get the words out of my mouth. I took one more moment to compose myself. "Will you kiss him and let him know I love him and that no matter what happens we are still going to work on forever." Latisha looked up at me one more time nodding, acknowledging what I had said and agreeing to do it for me. She stood up and began to walk into the ER when Naucia jumped out of my arms and proceeded to walk away from me and towards the hospital as well. "Where are you going?" I asked not knowing I was about to be blown away by my seven year old daughter. "Dad," she replied turning back around to look at me with a stern look on her face and attitude in her voice. "I think one of us needs to be in there for Daddy and since Jeremy isn't here and you can't go in, I will." In this moment of despair and sorrow, my seven year old daughter managed to bring a smile to my face, even if only for a short time. I was more proud of her today then I had ever been before. Not only is she accomplishing something that a normal seven year old could not even comprehend, she is accomplishing an adult task that even I couldn't do. Our family was united through all this and even Naucia seemed to see it.

The smile she had brought to my face continued as she turned and walked down the hallway of the hospital, Latisha's and her hands gripped tightly together. It was as if their hands had been together like that before and God had made them so that they would fit into each other's palms perfectly. Ericka's head still rested gently on my shoulder as my thoughts drifted back to Taylor, as I sat on the steps, my body numb unable to feel the cold temperature seeping in. I remember the great things he had done for this family, not only today but throughout his life. He provided and supported his family when I lost my job. He protected us from problems out of our control. He blessed us with his humor, patience and loving nature. I reminisced back onto some fun times. Like the time when we tried to give the family dog a bubble bath in the bathtub only to have him jump out splashing bubbles all over us. He then proceeded to run rampantly throughout the house making us chase his wet slippery body, dripping water and bubbles around the whole house. By the time we caught up to him he was practically dry, unlike ourselves. We all laughed as we dried up the water off the wood floors together. The smile began to slowly fade as I already started to miss him. I tried desperately to keep myself positive thru this praying that the trained doctors inside could save him, but as time went on my hope faded. Waiting to find out the news and expecting the worst, I tried to keep my mind off what the worst could actually be.

The whole time Erica just sat there not saying a word. She just held onto me tightly doing exactly what I needed her to do. Revisiting the past joys I had stored in the back of my mind for hard times like this was a new experience. I never needed them more than I did now. The mornings when I would wake up next to him lying in bed with me. The sun beaming in through the open window, the satin sheets thrown about from the night before, both of us intertwined with the other. The memories just reinforced the fact that sooner than later, I would be forced to wake up alone. I would have no one to hold or cuddle up with in the morning except our loving dog and kids. The time crept slowly for me, the waiting almost unbearable. The feeling of being left along was penetrating deeper and deeper into my soul as the time slowly went on. We did not move from the stair we were sitting on. Ericka's arms were still wrapped tightly around me. Her face planted in my chest.

After what seemed like an eternity, I felt a small gentle hand pressing down upon my shoulder. Naucia sat down next to me; the look on her face said it all. She curled up to my side giving Ericka and myself a big famous Naucia hug. Latisha stood behind us waiting for the right moment to give her condolences. "I'm sorry," she stated giving us all a moment to take it in. She informed me that she and Naucia had told Taylor everything that I had asked, holding his hand as they did. She also reassured me that they had done everything possible to try to revive him but that the wound was too great. "Come on," she urged, reminding me that I was supposed to be in the hospital as well. I had not been officially released and after the day I had I may need a few more days to recuperate. Helping me up we walked into the hospital together, the dreadful place that had started it all. I was placed back into the same room and in the same bed that I had woke up in earlier that day.

My eyes slammed shut the moment my head hit the same uncomfortable pillow, before I even had a chance to ask to see Taylor. "Come on girls, let's let your dad sleep," Latisha mentioned. They walked out holding each other's hands one girl on each side of her. Both of the girl's hands fit perfectly into hers. Their dark skin color matched perfectly, reminding Latisha of the two girls she once had. "I don't believe in coincidences," Latisha thought to herself as she recalled that today she had covered this very shift for one of her coworkers who desperately needed the day off. Had all this happened for a reason?

"You girls hungry?" She asked. The girls answered yes as they walked toward the exit of the emergency room turning down the hall and toward the cafeteria. Passing the nurses desk she noticed many media personnel surrounding them. "What are they doing here?" She asked another coworker, Naucia and Ericka's hands still firmly in hers. "They are getting the story of what happened today," one of the younger nurses replied excitedly, unaware of the hardships that had happened today. She had given her story and knew she was going to be on the news and quoted in tomorrow's paper. "They said it's going to be front page news," the young nurse said arrogantly. She had obviously not been through what Latisha had today and she did not get it. She did not understand that front page news tomorrow was someone else's tragic story today.

Chapter 11

    My eyes rolled open after what seemed like only minutes. My body ached as the confusion as to where I was crept in. My body lay on the bed weak and for the most part motionless. My tongue wet my lips. The beeping of a heart monitor sounded to the side of me. Beeping periodically letting me know I was still alive. The sound of the toilet flushing grabbed my attention. My eyes rolled over to a black woman exiting the restroom. "Oh! You're awake?" She said in a more stunned voice than I thought she should have used, confused to why she was here or why I was here for that matter. "How are you feeling?" She asked as she ran up to the side of my bed Jeremy joining her from the other side of the room shortly after. I was in slight confusion from looking at him. Fake pearls dangled down from her ears and a pearl necklace hung around her neck. The purple shirt she wore illuminated and brightened her skin just perfectly. The choice of clothes covering her excess weight well. I looked at an older looking Jeremy for explanation wondering what the hell was going on. Grabbing my hand and lifting it up to hers, she gripped tightly pressing my hand up against her heart. It was as if it were the first time seeing me in a long time or perhaps the last time she would see me before a long goodbye. I looked to Jeremy confused as to why everything about him had changed.

    She looked ravishing, although I could not see her entire outfit, her eyes brightened with a perfect hint of purple shadow and her hair gently framing her face, still confused to exactly who she was. Unable to speak from the lack of energy, she took it upon herself to fill the silence. She asked questions about my body and how I was feeling, confusing me with each additional question. Unaware that she had pushed the button signaling the nurses working the floor, two nurses a male and a female, opened the door and paced their way across the room toward me. They began checking vital signs and repeating the questions that the black woman had already asked, as I looked over at her and our eyes meet. I had a feeling that she had something to tell me both her and Jeremy, but what could they have to say. As the male nurse lifted my arm to move the tubes out of the way, I began to notice more.

The white sleeve of a hospital gown hanging off my arm shown from the corner of my vision. The tubes and needles attached to my body were feeding me and keeping me alive. My mind began to wonder. What had happened to put me in this state I thought? I glanced back to the black woman, looking up at her for answers. I only received an incomprehensive stare back. A stare full of information she needed to release; information that she needed to let me know and information she needed to gain herself. I could tell that she wanted to tell someone but couldn't, she had to hold this in for me. She could not tell anyone, until she told me. But how long was she going to hold this in, how long had she been holding it in already? The nurses continued to manipulate and maneuver my body and the machines attached to it as my eyes shifted back and forth from Jeremy's to hers. Still unable to talk, I just nodded or shook my head to the questions that the nurses were asking. Latisha's anticipation and eagerness for the other nurses to leave became noticeable. The look of frustration was evident in her face as she began pushing them to hurry until they actually turned and walked toward the door. She stared at the door waiting for it to close. As soon as it clicked shut, she began to talk.

Before she could get too far into her story I looked at

104

Jeremy again and rudely interrupted asking him what was going on and who this woman was. After being upset that I didn't remember who she was she began telling me everything that had happened. She informed me that Jeremy approved the hospital to put me in a medically induced coma; they said it would help my brain heal properly and was the only way that I would not suffer any more damage then I already had. My jaw dropped and anger set in as I heard her continue to tell me everything. I could not believe it. It was all so unreal. Was I dreaming? Was this all actually happening? I lay there confused. There is no possible way that this could have happened. The woman stepped forward to place her hand on mine once again and said, "I'm in this for the long haul. Don't think I'm giving up on you." I looked at Jeremy nodding in agreement conforming that it was all true, before looking back at the woman I supposedly knew as Latisha trying to piece anything from my mind together. "Thank you," I said in a raspy but solid voice confused as to what exactly I was saying thank you for and why she was in this for the long haul, and what exactly it was.

After bickering back and forth for quite some time I let her question me about parts of the story to see if anything had stuck. Latisha knew that the coma I had just woken up from definitely affected my memory and may be permanent. After coming to the conclusion that I really did not remember much of the last few weeks, she agreed to tell me the story again. "Shortly after I brought you into your hospital room and put you in this bed the doctors decided that because of all the trauma you had been through the other day we needed to let your body rest and let your brain relax from its swollen damaged state. Taylor's parents came a few days after he passed to take his body. Along with his body they also took Naucia and Ericka." My facial expressions changed dramatically to a confused state. I had so many questions to ask her and she would not give me a chance to ask, she just kept talking. "Taylor's parents said to me that, it was better this way. The kids need a good home with stability and good role models from a mother and a father. Since Taylor did not leave a will and you are not the legal adoptive father, there was nothing I could do but let them take your children. I have been looking in the local newspaper daily to save Taylor's obituary for you but I have not come across one. I'm assuming they just did not care to pay for one." "Wait a second," I said, rudely interrupting her. "Taylor's dead?"

"Yes," she said calmly and confused. "He was shot by the police. You were standing right there in front of him. You held his body as he died." Tears streamed down my face. This was the first time I had heard this or so I thought. "You're wrong," I yelled back at her as I looked to the older looking Jeremy for confirmation. "None of this happened. You're lying." I screamed at them confused as to why they were telling me these lies. "Who are you? How do you know what happened to him?" I screamed out in pain. "Latisha, the nurse that helped you save him, and your kids." She said. "You didn't help me save him. You just said he was dead," I yelled back frustrated at all of this. "Look," she said upset that I didn't remember. She took the newspaper off of the night stand and put it in front of me with the headline on the front page reading "Man Unnecessarily Shot and Killed." After reading the article, I put my head in my hands trying to calm down, Jeremy rubbing my back trying to comfort me as much as he could as I tried to think back and remember anything that the nurse said had happened. "The last thing I remember was Taylor, Jeremy and me playing football on the front lawn," I said utterly confused.

As I lay there thinking about Taylor and Jeremy the story she had just told me kept replaying. I tried to piece it all together. "Naucia and Ericka. Who are they?" I asked Latisha. My head was still firmly in my hands. My eyes closed as I tried to focus. "Excuse me?" Latisha said, not understanding why I would even consider asking that question, Jeremy's face all the while in frustration at the situation and my lack of memory. "The two girls you mentioned in the story, the ones that we saved from the old people at the school. Who are they?" Latisha obviously stunned by my question just stood there unresponsive. Moments passed as the expression on her face became concerned and saddened. "You don't remember Naucia and Ericka?" She asked. "No," I responded in an angry tone. I was not sure why these two girls were so important to the story or how I would even know them and more importantly why we wasted time getting to them instead of saving Taylor. "They're your children," she replied, staring up at me. 'No," I said shaking my head. "No, we only have Jeremy I said pointing toward him. Taylor and I never adopted any girls, just Jeremy. We were planning on it, but never did." Tears started flowing from my eyes. I thought about all the future plans that Taylor and I had together. Latisha stood there concerned. She debated what was best for the girls. Should they stay with Taylor's parents that could raise them well? Or should they be with a man that once loved them but now has no clue who they even are?

After taking a few moments to myself, taking all of the information in, I looked back at Latisha and asked, "There is one more thing I don't understand." "What's that?" She replied wondering what she had not fully explained. "Why are you helping me? Why are you doing this?" "Like I have told you before I once had children of my own, two girls actually, they were beautiful. In the beginning of all of this, I was not sure exactly what we had in common or why I was helping you. But now after going through this short journey with you, I see why I was put in this position." She said sitting down on the edge of the bed next to me Jeremy standing behind her. "I see why I was

107

sent here to help you," she said continuing to respond to my question. "My two girls were taken from me as well. I unfortunately do not know where they are or who they are with. You on the other hand know exactly who has them and we are going to fight to get them back. Taylor's' parents do not love them. You do." Tears began to develop in her eyes. "I have been searching for my girls for years and it has been hell every day. Every day that goes by is another day that they may assume their mother did not want them or that I was not looking for them. I promise you it will not take you years. We will find your kids and get them back."

She decided to tell me her whole story so that I could fully understand. She started in the beginning from when her first child was born and then to how they were taken. I lay back and rested my head against the pillow and drifted off slightly. I put myself in her shoes as she told me the story. "I kissed both of my girls and hugged them tight before turning and walking out of our home in the village. I had a long walk ahead of me and I knew it. I had walked that trail for a few months and I was beginning to get used to it. The few miles did not seem as far as it did the first few times. Although it was far and took hours, I knew it was all worth it. I was making a better life for my girls. This opportunity was not given to just anyone in my African village. I earned this internship and I was not going to ruin it. I continued walking almost out of sight from the house. I turned back as I did every day to wave at my girls standing in the doorway waving and wishing me luck. The walk was long but it gave me time to think. Mostly I thought about the future. How amazing it was going to be when I got a job from this schooling and how the income would be able to help my family have a much better and safer life."

"Not many people in Africa have jobs or an amazing one

at that, but I will, I thought. The doctor I helped knew how far I walked to get to the small hospital. He knew how committed I was. I was for sure going to get a job when they needed me. As I walked in the office every day I would greet people, say hello and make my way down to the small hospital area I worked in. We injected vaccines and talked to locals and tried to help cure them of whatever it was that was ailing them. Dr. Bradley would tell me stories of what it was like back in America and how things were so much different. Africa was all I knew but his stories fascinated me. He would talk for hours without me saying a word. I only nodded my head to let him know I was listening and to please keep going. I never stopped smiling when I was there; I enjoyed his stories and the experiences too much. Occasionally my mind would drift off to the thought of what my children were doing at home with my grandmother and I would wish I was there with them.

The shifts were long and tiresome. I worked 10-14 hours a day, all for the hope of a possible job when the internship was all over. Dr. Bradley was there in our hospital on a grant and not even he knew when it was going to run out. Then one night the walk home seemed very different. All I remember was this awful feeling that hit me when I saw my grandmother sitting on top of the little hill by our house. I ran toward her knowing something was terribly wrong. She looked up at me and said, "They're gone." "The happiness from earlier fell to the ground along with my heart. "What do you mean they're gone?" I remember asking afraid to hear the answer. She shook her head still trying to piece together what had happened. "The men, the men," she tried to stumble out. "The men. They came out of a large white van as the kids were playing in the street. I was inside preparing dinner for them and I heard screaming. I dropped everything and rushed outside. The moment I did, all I saw were two men throwing Nyaga in the back of the van and drive off. I ran after them trying to follow the tire tracks, but I couldn't. The tracks mixed in with others already in the road. I asked people if they had seen a large white van but no one had. I searched all day until just now when I came up here to wait for you." My grandmother said. My eyes opened as Latisha took a moment. I lay there in bed. Tears began to fall after looking at her. I felt guilty for making her tell this story, but at the same time intrigued to hear the rest. After a few more moments had passed Latisha looked up and said, "I don't tell a lot of people this story. I just feel that you need to hear it." I nodded my head in agreement letting her know that I understood. "Take as much time as you need," I said.

A few more moments passed before she began her story once again. "I was exhausted from the long day in the hospital but I kept running. Village to village, I ran asking people if they had seen a white van or knew of anyone that did. I looked for it myself as well. I searched through the night checking every village around us. I knew I shouldn't have been out in the villages at night. I knew this time I was upset enough that I could fight off anyone. Even if I couldn't, at this point I did not care. These were my children and that is all that mattered. Both of my girls came from situations of being out at night and getting raped. My grandmother knew that. I am sure she was frightened for me and afraid that it would happen once again, but she understood. She knew I was their mother and it was what I had to do. I never made it home that night. Honestly I was not sure where I went." My eyes were wide open. I was intrigued by the story. I became mesmerized as to how she even made it through the night. "I remember the sunlight radiating up over the horizon casting shadows across the vast desert I was in. I began making my way toward the hospital not wanting to give up on the opportunity I had there. I was far away from my home. I could not remember a time I had ever been out that far. I was not sure how long it

110

would take me to get back, so I began walking. I know that children get taken from the streets all the time. I just never thought that it would ever be mine. I was exhausted and my legs were tired. My stomach was twisted but I was not hungry. My body was weak and I could feel the lack of energy and nutrition that I had.

My motivation and adrenaline were the only things keeping me on my feet. It kept me going. I eventually made it to the hospital. Practically crawling in through the front doors, the rest of the hospital personnel just stared. Afraid to ask what had happened, they knew that nothing that happened here was ever good. Looking up at the clock, I realized that I was late. I was afraid that this may put my future job at risk. Dr. Bradley looked at me as I entered the room. My body looked pale and exhausted. Even though I had drunk water in the break room moments before, I was dehydrated and Dr. Bradley could see that. He stopped what he was doing, put down the tools and walked over to me. My nerves got to me. I was sure he was going to tell me that I was late and unpredictable and that he did not need me anymore. But he did not. Instead he cared. He asked me what happened, as tears flowed down my face. I could see in his expressions that he was astounded and in disbelief that this could happen. Especially to someone he knew and cared about. As I continued talking his expressions changed. They moved from concerned to confused to curious.

"Did you say there were two girls?" He asked me unsure of why he was asking. "Yeah, why?" I responded still confused. He looked puzzled as if he was trying to think deeply about something. "Do either of your daughters' have a Mongolian spot on their neck?" He asked slightly questioning his reasoning of asking. "Yes, Nyaga my oldest had quite a large one on the front side of her neck. How did you know?" I said. My face lit up

111

unexpectedly surprised but for some reason happy that he knew. "I think your daughters' were here earlier today," he said. I shot up to my feet interrupting him. "What? Why?" I screamed at him.

"There were two older men. They claimed the girls needed their shots and proof of documentation so they could be adopted to someone in America." "What? Adopted?" I yelled back frustrated and angry that this was happening. "Yes. As I was going through the normal routine and trying to make casual conversation, I inquired of the two men as to who the girls were being adopted by and where they were taking them now. I am not sure if they were telling me the truth or not," Dr. Bradley said. "They said they had a nice couple waiting to see the girls and take them home, just a few villages away."

"So how did you end up over here?" I asked Latisha as she readjusted herself on the edge of my hospital bed. "The doctor, Dr. Bradley," she said curious if I remembered who he was, not sure if I was listening or could even remember after all I had been through. "After hearing my story and trying to help me find them by driving me to all the nearby villages that my girls could have possibly been taken to, we finally gave up. We knew that after those few days of searching, they had probably already flown here to the United States with the family that adopted them."

I nodded my head to let her know I was paying attention as she continued. "He informed me that because of all my hard work and efforts in volunteering at the hospital, he was going to make some calls and get me a place to stay and a job at the hospital here in town. He knew where they said they were sending my girls to; he remembered the city where the family supposedly lived. It was a long shot but all we could do was hope and pray that the city that the two men told Dr. Bradley they were being adopted to was actually where they were taken. He rushed me to the airport and a few hours later I was in the air on my first airplane ride, on my way to America, without a chance to even say goodbye to my grandmother. I was in flight unsure of what to expect and not knowing where I was even going." She looked back at me as tears rolled down her cheeks. "I have been here ever since. Looking and searching for them. Hoping that one day I might find them. So yeah," she said. "I know how you feel." "I had no idea." I said. My eyes full of emotion from listening to the story of her journey. "I can't even imagine," I said as I gazed up at her with compassion. "Oh do not worry," she replied "You are about to experience a journey of your own."

After Latisha questioned me for what seemed like longer than necessary, we established that I did not remember anything over the past 2-3 years. Not Latisha. Not the girls. Not even Taylor's death. I did not remember any of it. All I could do was try and force myself to relearn it. I read the front page of the newspaper. It presented me with the story of what Taylor had done and how he died trying.

The next day Latisha and Jeremy walked in with a box in his arms full of items from our house that she thought might help me remember the last few years. "Did you find some things that may help," I questioned, as they walked toward the bed. "I think so," Jeremy interjected in a hopeful tone. Jeremy pulled up two chairs to the side of the bed and placed the box on the ground in front of her. She talked to me for a few moments reminding me that we agreed to do this together, something to try and ignite past memories. She explained where Jeremy had actually gotten the stuff in the box from reassuring me that it was all very real. They started off showing me a family picture with all of us in it. Taylor and me standing in the back proud of our family we loved.

Surrounded by our three kids, Jeremy who looked much older than I had remembered him, but younger than he did now. Also the two girls that were apparently part of our family even though I still did not remember, standing on both sides of Jeremy. I stared deeply into that picture. I tried to remember anything that would help remind me of the girls or the last few years but nothing came.

She reached into the box again and pulled out a few more items. She stressed to me that these items were actually from my home and of the love that Taylor and I shared before she pulled out a picture of just Naucia and Ericka. They were lying on the sand at the beach, the water rushing over them as they laughed. "Look," I said proud pointing at the picture forgetting that they were my girls. "That girl has the same mark you said your daughter had." Latisha immediately pulled the picture back toward her and sat back into her chair as she stared at it. She ignored the beautiful silver frame around it, only focusing on the mark and the two girls faces. Her eyes became fixated on the picture. "When did you adopt these girls?" She asked looking up at me, and then back at Jeremy, neglecting the fact that I did not even know they were mine, far less the day I supposedly adopted them. She realized I had no clue with the confused look that I had on my face. She rummaged through the box frantically looking for something specific. She pulled out a folder full of papers. Flipping through each paper individually, I asked "What is that?" "The adoption papers for your girls," she replied. Her eyes were still centered on looking through the stack of stapled papers and not so much on my questions. "Well, can I see them?" I asked, seeing that I was the one we were trying to get to remember things. She said nothing as she kept rummaging through the papers, then stopped suddenly. She stared at the page intently, her eyes flashing from side to side reading the material in search of something. "What is it," Jeremy questioned.

Her eyes stopped. Her face turned empty, in complete disbelief as she looked back at our picture of the girls.

"What is it?" I asked, this time waiting for an answer confused by the whole situation and starting to get slightly upset. Latisha looked up at me with an amazed look on her face. "These are my girls." She said. In a moment where I should have been happy for her I was not. I was getting more frustrated with her. "I thought we are talking about my family? And if they are your girls, why are they in a family picture with us?" "Remember when you asked how I got here? Why I was helping you? And I told you that my girls were stolen from me back in Africa and sold to someone in America. I never knew the reason why I felt I should help you. That was very unlike me. Something told me I should. It was them. These are my daughters. They sold them to you and Taylor." "Taylor and I never adopted girls. We only adopted Jeremy." "No Dad she's right." Jeremy said knowing all well that he had two sisters. "See, look!" She yelled, as she stood up and shoved the adoption papers in my face. "Here is the date you adopted them, three days after they were taken from me. Here is Taylor's signature proving that he is the adoptive father." She yelled pointing out each place Taylor had signed before hurling the box to the floor and walking out in frustration as Jeremy chased out of the room after her. There was nothing I could do. I did not have enough energy to sit up on my own far less chase after her. All I could do was lie here in bed confused; I closed my eyes and tried to think. I tried to remember anything about the girls, as I slowly fell asleep.

Chapter 12

We had not seen Latisha for weeks after she had walked out furious that her girls were literally in her arms and taken away once again. Every night before I would fall asleep I would put the newspaper with Taylor's article on my nightstand. It reminded me to read it again each morning hoping I would finally remember what had happened. After reading the now wrinkled paper I would go through the box of items taken from our home and ask Jeremy to retell me everything that had happened along with some happy memories from the time that I had mentally lost. I would stare blankly into the pictures of our family that I did not even recognize. I only had memories of Taylor and the first few years with Jeremy, I could not remember anything of the girls Latisha claimed were at one point hers but also mine. As the days went on I grew less and less frustrated at my memory loss and more on the situation as a whole. I recognized that it happened and there was nothing I could do about it. I missed Taylor deeply but I knew I had to stay strong. I still had a family waiting out there for me and expecting me to fight to get them back home. Family is family I thought, and Jeremy agreed. He was the man now and he knew what he was going to have to do.

Other nurses would come in to care for me but none of them were as friendly or as compassionate as Latisha was from what all they had told me, not remembering her service or generosity myself. They only did their job. They would put on a fake smile and then leave as fast as they had come. I would ask the other nurses occasionally if they had seen or heard from Latisha. Each time I would receive the same heartless answer of no. I was worried about Latisha, where she was and what she was doing. I knew that this could not have been easy for her. Every day as I would think about her, I planned all of the things I was going to say. I needed to thank her for all she had done. Even though she may still be mad at me, she deserved my thanks and my sincere apology. I went through every item in the box a few times daily continuing to find new questions to ask Jeremy. He was very diligent and stayed in my room with me on a roll in cot that the hospital provided us. He would sit by my side everyday helping me recover as best I could, quizzing me daily on the topics and questions we had answered the day before. I even got to meet his girlfriend Stacy the few times that I was awake when she would come to visit. I was literally seeing my little boy grow up in front of me. At this point I practically had every note and every photo memorized. I did not know if I was beginning to remember the girls and our experiences with them, or was I just creating memories based off of the photos I kept looking at daily? I would flip through page after page of our family photo album, stalling on each page for minutes at a time. I looked through all the papers and legal documents for our ring ceremony and our adoption papers for Jeremy.

As I would look at Jeremy's papers and look back at the pictures, I would remember the girls adoption papers Latisha had shown me a few weeks before. I would search the box for them. I even asked the nurses and Jeremy if they had fallen under the bed because I could not find them anywhere. I assumed she took them with her but I was not honestly sure why. The days went by slowly. I rested and slept through most of it. I lay there day after day, hour after hour. Sporadically, I would hear a knock on the door. I hoped to see Latisha standing in the doorway but every time it was only the nurse, or Jeremy coming back from the cafeteria with food or a movie for us to watch. I enjoyed all the time I was able to spend with Jeremy but without Taylor here I was as lonely as ever. I prayed each night before I would fall asleep that the next day would be better. After a few weeks, I was able to sit up on my own, turn the TV on and watch the morning news without Jeremy's help, giving him more time alone to rest, without me asking him a thousand questions. Today I followed the same routine. After watching the weather man reiterate the local weather for the third or fourth time, there was a knock on the door. A knock much quicker than the rest I had heard. Looking at the clock on the wall I thought it could not have been time for the morning nurse to be here already. I stared at the door waiting to see who it was on the other side. I could not see anything through the small hospital room window covered in papers. My heart was racing as Jeremy awoke. The door handle slowly turned downward further and further until it clicked at the bottom fully unlocked. I waited for pressure from the other side to open the door into my room.

The crack in the door emerged and expanded blowing open as Naucia and Ericka ran like angels toward me. Landing on the bed they wrapped their arms around me and squeezed tighter than ever. Love and emotions were exchanged. Both of them expressed how much they missed me and loved me. All I could do was return the feelings having become accustom to the idea of being their father. I looked up to see Latisha standing in the doorway with a large smile on her face knowing what she had done was right. I motioned with my head for her to come over and participate in this joyous reunion. As she sat on the edge of the bed, the girls lifted their heads off my shoulder to look me in the eyes. They had no idea I had forgotten they were mine. They were like the missing puzzle piece to my memory. The love, the trips, the tears, the fun, it all came creeping back slowly and Latisha could tell what was happening. She smiled once again bigger than I had seen her smile before in the short time I had known her. She was utterly happy and content with her life at that precise moment. She had done what she had promised. She could see and feel its reward.

I was overwhelmed and unable to say anything. I wanted to thank her for what she had done but I was at that moment completely speechless. I had to stay in the hospital for another few days. Our girls stayed right there with me playing games or telling me stories of what we used to do sleeping at night here in the room, one on my bed and one on Jeremy's cot with him. Their stories helped me remember the past. Latisha stayed as much as she could enjoying her time with them once again. When the girls would go down to the cafeteria with Jeremy to get lunch or dinner, it gave Latisha and me a few minutes alone to discuss the things she had done over the last few weeks since she had walked out. She informed me that she hired a lawyer and gave him all of our adoptive documents for the girls. She told him the story she had told me and explained how they were actually hers. The adoption agency Taylor and I used was apparently a fake. It had been shut down early last year after being caught in the act of stealing and selling children. The girls were forced to do a DNA test to prove her story. After the test came back proving that Naucia and Ericka were biologically hers she told me that she had a very difficult time deciding what she should do next. She was happy to have her girls back but neither of them knew who she was, they longed for their father. Her girls were back in her life but she was not happy.

She told me how she contemplated keeping her two girls to herself and never bringing them back to me. However she said she realized that it was not my fault this happened. Despite it being unfair for her, I had nothing to do with it. Taylor and I just wanted children to love. Taylor and I did not steal them from her. We were just two loving parents that wanted to help and nurture two children that needed a home. She knew that we had not only given them a better life but what we also gave her a chance at life in America. I thanked her for bringing them back to me along with thanking her for all that she had done for my family. We both decided not to tell them all that had happened. That she was their biological mother. We agreed that she would stay around as a family friend as much as possible. Having done so much for this family I really did consider her just that, family. We agreed that when the girls were slightly older we would explain what all had happened and how they had ended up in both of our lives.

I told her that whenever they let me out of here, I wanted to see Taylor's grave and asked if she would take me. A week later she and the girls wheeled me out to her same old beat up car, placed me in the front seat and we drove away from that wretched hospital. I looked back at that hospital as we exited the emergency room and thought of the harm that place had caused my family because of one simple rule. I told myself that I was going to do everything in my power to fight for our rights and make sure that this never happened to another soul. We drove to the grave yard under the direction of the girls since they were the only ones that had actually been there before.

The cold winter wind blew at my face as I rolled down my window, my tears swelling in my eyes. Latisha stopped the car on the top row of the cemetery against the fence next to the public road. Naucia pointed to the ground up against the fence that still had the uprooted grass rectangle outlining where the casket had gone. Latisha took both of the girl's hands and walked them off to the other side of the grave yard, giving me time to be alone with Taylor. Time that I very much needed and she knew that. I stared down at the unmarked grave site with no proof that Taylor's body actually lay there. I knelt down on the frozen frosty ground near Taylors supposed body. "Taylor," I said still unsure if he was even there, as tears flowed down my face almost crystallizing before falling like ice cubes to the ground. "Taylor," I said again forcing the words out of my mouth, "Love of my life. Thank you. Thank you for everything. For our loving kids, for supporting us through the hard times, for loving us each passing day, you fought to protect us and comfort us up to your very last day. I will never forget what you have done for me and our family. You truly have been the most marvelous father to our children and a loving husband, partner and soul mate to me. I will love you forever. This is not the end. It is just the beginning. Just like you always said, "It's about the memory of what's behind and the promise of what's ahead." Tears fell as I pulled out a letter that was in the box of stuff Latisha and Jeremy had brought me in the hospital. It was a letter that Taylor once wrote to me and I wanted to read it back to him at this particular moment. I cleared my throat before I started talking:

"Bryan,

I love you with all my heart and wouldn't have it any other way. You truly are the light of my life and I know that you are the one for me Bryan. We are meant to be and you know it as much as I know it. You truly make me happy and so grateful that I have you to be by my side. Last night was a very hard night but we pulled through again. You are the love of my life and I'm excited to go on this journey with you till the end. I love you my Bry, my beautiful boy.

Always,

Taylor'

121

"This is not the end Taylor," I added after finishing the letter. "This is just the beginning of forever." By this time the letter was filled with even more tear spots than it had received from previous times that I had read it. Latisha and the girls walked up shortly after I had stood up. Holding and comforting me, Latisha knew that this couldn't have been easy. "Let's go home," I said, ready to be back in the place I felt most comfortable. At the same time I was afraid that everything there would remind me of Taylor. I knew eventually I would have to face it, but I felt him nearby, somewhere in my heart saying he would always be with me, comforting me and continuing to show his undying love. After offering and pleading with Latisha to move into our home, she accepted a few days later. She realized that she wanted to be closer to the girls but also financially she was barely getting by after her split from her husband. I also needed much more help around the house now that Taylor was gone, and I was still recuperating. We had an extra room, the one that my grandmother had once stayed in. It was only fitting that this special woman stays in the same room now.

Almost a year passed and Thanksgiving arrived once more. We all sat around the dining room table surrounded by loving family and friends. As we did every year we prepared for the toasts by pouring fresh glasses of wine and sparkling cider for the kids. Jeremy was the first to stand up and give a toast obviously excited to say something. I recalled that usually he was the very last to say anything. We generally had to force him to give one at all. Maybe it was because his girlfriend Stacy was at the table with us or maybe it was just because he was actually grateful this year. Either way I was proud of him, so I sat upright and listened.

"This last year has been rough for all of us, from dad's

death to being torn away from our family. Although I claimed I wanted to move out and leave this house when I turned 18, I realized when presented with the choice to do so and leave this house I couldn't. I realized that the only place I wanted to be was here. I wanted to be here, where I was loved, and where I feel that love. Bryan, you have been the best father I could ever imagine and I thank you for that. Latisha," he said turning to raise his glass to her. "You have done more for our family than anyone should ever have to do, even more than I could ever see myself doing for someone that I didn't even know. For all that you have done for this family, I have something for you." Stacy handed him a silver box no bigger than a stack of envelopes, wrapped with bows that even Taylor would approve of. The look of surprise on her face was priceless. She was caught off guard not prepared or expecting to receive a gift.

She opened her beautiful very gay looking box and peeked inside. She revealed our family portrait with herself photo shopped in flawlessly, standing as part of our family. On that beautiful Thanksgiving night, we all raised our glasses ready to say cheers as Jeremy finished his speech. "We are all together in the end," he said still looking at Latisha. "And you are always welcome here. A place without judgment, a place full of love and laughter." And as he finished his toast he quoted the words engraved on the frame of the family portrait that Latisha had just opened. "All of us together, Together as One."

The End

About The Author

OLIVERI PHOTOGRAPHY

Author of "The Unprotected" Ryan Ford continues to fight toward equality and equal rights for all

Ford has been fighting for equality in his home state of Utah, as well as his home in California and across the nation since he came out in 2007. Protesting at equality events such as the Proposition 8 protests and humbling himself at numerous candle light vigils for LGBT suicides. The book is dedicated to those men, women, and children that have lost the battle to live, which includes his loving boyfriend who passed suddenly in 2009.

A hometown boy of Farmington, UT and 2007 Viewmont High School Graduate, Ford has had an amazing and intriguing start to his career and beginning of his new life as a Gay Man. As an author and Gay Rights activist, Ford has established himself as a future leader in the fight for Equality. From Publishing to assisting and comforting other LGBT individuals in their journey of acceptance, Ford has proudly deemed himself a lifesaver.

Ford grew up around the areas of Salt Lake City, and attended The Church of Jesus Christ of Latter Day Saints, Farmington 3rd ward. A faithful attendant until September of 2007, when instead of going on a LDS Mormon Mission he accepted his life and came out as a gay man never to look back.

For more information "Like" Facebook.com/RyanFordFanPage

www.ingramcontent.com/pod-product-compliance
Lightning Source LLC
Chambersburg PA
CBHW060400290526
45791CB00002B/573